The Holistic Christian Woman

A Healthy Journey through the Fruit of the Spirit

Spiritually
Emotionally
Physically

Cynthia Damaskos, CHC

ISBN: 978-0986129209

Printed in the United States of America

Dedication

To Nun Gavrilia, who, through her book, *The Ascetic of Love*, introduced me to Mother Gavrilia. Someone who has continued to influence and inspire me each time I read her biography. I pray more people will read her beautiful book, which is obviously a labor of love.

An Introduction to Mother Gavrilia

For those of you who are not familiar with Mother Gavrilia, I would like to give you a brief introduction.

Born in 1897 to a highly respected, wealthy family in Constantinople, she became the second woman to enter into a Greek university. She studied botany in Switzerland and philosophy in Thessaloniki. Not only smart and well educated, she also had a great sense of humor. However, it was her great love for others that made her the woman God could use. Always following His will, she worked in many capacities in many countries but it was when she became a physiotherapist, with a specialty in conditions of the feet, that He opened up the rest of the world to her. She was 49 at that time. Mother's favorite saying was, "Through the feet to the heart."

At the point in her life when many would be looking forward to retiring, and a life of leisure, she was just getting started. She chose to live in poverty and hardship while traveling the world, and worked alongside people of all faiths and cultures. It wasn't the life that she was born into, but she wanted to be where the pain was. She wanted to love others so much that God could use her to heal them. And that is exactly what happened. Her listening skills were so developed, that people only needed to talk to her to experience relief, physically, and psychologically.

One of the aspects of her Faith that has always struck me, was her ability to say yes to opportunities, and trust that God would lead her wherever He wanted her. When she was presented with an opportunity, she always said yes, and then left it in His hands. She is a tremendous example of how God can take one person and, if they are willing, mold them into the person that He wants them to be. And yet, despite her conviction that she must always say "yes," I find it interesting that she turned down all of opportunities that would have made her rich and famous. They were opportunities that others may have eagerly accepted as a blessing, and a sign from God, that they were on the right path. And yet, she had discernment. She knew the path that God had for her, and knew when an opportunity was a temptation in disguise.

After getting to know her in these pages, you may want to know more about this extraordinary example of love in action. If this is the case, I encourage you to read *The Ascetic Of Love*.

Table of Contents

Acknowledgements vi

Foreword viii

Introduction xiii

First Things First 1

Love 13

Joy... 29

Peace... 41
    By Molly Sabourin

Longsuffering 57
    By Elise Adams

Kindness.. 67

Goodness.. 79

Faithfulness 91

Gentleness 105

Self-control.. 119
    By Rita Madden

Conclusion.. 132
    How to Hire a Health Coach

Acknowledgements

One of my co-workers, who became a good friend, used to tell me that it's all about me. As in, "Yes Cynthia, it's all about you, isn't it?" As a nod to his jesting, while I will be sharing a lot of personal stories, I have included chapters with contributions from friends. I've encouraged them to share of themselves and the wisdom they have acquired so that it isn't all about me, since now I have a phobia.

I would like to thank Molly Sabourin, Rita Madden and Elise Adams for their contributions, and take this time to introduce them to you.

Molly Maddex Sabourin is a professional photographer, freelance writer and speaker. She is a regular podcaster for Ancient Faith Radio with her podcast called "Close to Home," and is a wife and mother of four. Her first book, *Close to Home*, has become a source of comfort and inspiration to many. She always inspires me with her warmth and humor, and I love that I can share her with you in this book. You can read more of Molly's work on her blog at blogs.ancientfaith.com/closetohome, and can experience her beautiful photography on the website, www.mollysabourin.com.

Rita Madden (MPH, RD) enjoys consulting with people who are eager to manage and prevent chronic diseases and lose weight through a faith-based approach to eating and living. She is a Registered Dietician who finds inspiration in the great role that the Christian faith plays in her modern day health care profession. Rita teaches at the university level, provides over the phone and web-based consulting, and is a professional speaker, who lectures on bringing balance to the body through natural ways of eating and living. She also has a popular podcast on Ancient Faith Radio called "Food, Faith and Fasting." I'm so glad to share the wisdom of this treasured friend who epitomizes for me what the holistic Christian woman is all about. I can't wait for her upcoming book, which I will no doubt be giving to all of my clients!

Elise Photini Adams is an inspiration of hope for anyone who has ever felt hopeless. After experiencing homelessness, addiction, and abuse, she has been able to "reinvent" her life not only once, but several times, when many would have given up. Using Christian principals and embracing the life of the Church, she gives others hope through her victories. There are a lot of theories out there, but a personal "been there done that, survived then thrived" message of personal experience is what connects her deeply to people. "I'm not afraid to share the real journey, the struggle that we all share. It's the life of the church, not just the theory or theology that saves me. And I can't help but keep sharing." I'm so happy that Elise's experiences are a part of this book and that she can lift you up, as she has lifted me up, on a number of occasions!

Foreword

I t all started in church. I had always heard that the biggest changes in life can come when you feel like you have bottomed out. I was definitely at that point, and it had been coming for a few months. The sermon that day was about living out your faith, and that what you believe is what your life reflects. If your life does not reflect what you think or say your beliefs are, you need to reevaluate yourself and your life.

I've heard that before, as many of us have, and you nod your head yes, in agreement. It just doesn't seem to apply to you for some reason. Either you feel like you are living out your faith and your values or someone else just comes to mind instead of yourself.

But that day, I was sitting there with the weight of the world on my shoulders, the inability to concentrate, the inability to have fun doing things that I used to have fun doing, and feeling like I was truly lost, and my life was out of control. God, is this really how you want me to live? We all know the answer.

For me, I think it was a mixture of wanting to be everything to everybody, and no doubt some hormonal dysfunction. I bring up hormones because my mind had become less focused, and I was unable to concentrate on things that were truly important. I could be wrong but I don't think in my younger years I would have considered myself as spacey or flighty, but yes, that was exactly how feared I had become. Do you feel like you are a different person from what you used to be?

For some odd reason, one of my ways of coping was to spend my free time wandering around stores, browsing at items that I didn't need, and ultimately buying something on my way out. This was destructive not only from a time management perspective, but also from a financial standpoint. Obviously my intentions of trying to be everything to everybody did not cross over to the stress that I was causing my husband by buying things that we really didn't need. Can you relate to shopping as comfort or therapy? Maybe you don't have the resources to make mindless shopping your mini vacation. Other women I know immerse themselves in books or television, whenever they can, to escape their sense of overwhelm.

The sermon really hit me that day. My life was mine to change. I could create in it anything I'd ever wanted, and could live out my beliefs and priorities without being tossed around by the wind. As long as I stuck with it, this could be the answer to a life of barely keeping my head above water, to living life abundantly.

I love the word "abundantly." I always have although I could never identify with it, and thought that it was only a term that could be used by other people. Are you familiar with Dr. Cindy Trimm? She is a bestselling author, former senator, and has great inspirational videos on YouTube and her website. When I see her, I think, abundant! I'll have what she's having!

That day in church is when I decided that I needed to back out of some things that I was doing to make other people happy, but were no longer fun or fulfilling to me. There were friends who offered to help me through this difficult time by taking over a couple of my volunteer responsibilities, thereby freeing me up to help redesign my world. While the roles I had accepted were easy, and may not have taken up much time by themselves, when you put ten things together, it can take up more time than you have to give. These seemingly innocuous commitments add up. They take up mental space, memory capabilities and time management skills that you may not be able to tap into when you're totally tapped out! Have you had this same issue? Saying yes to more than you can handle? I know women with children are put in this position constantly.

Some decisions were hard to make, like not driving to Chicago for church every Sunday and choosing to stay local. I had put off the difficult decision for eight years, and giving it up gave me eight or nine hours more to my week when all was said and done. Just making this very difficult decision and feeling the instant lightness inspired me to make other less difficult time management decisions. Maybe that is the key. Is there one really huge thing that you are holding onto that you never thought could be let go?

I can do all things through Christ who strengthens me. ~Philippians 4:13

Of course, the mere fact that this revelation happened in church was not just a coincidence, or some inspiration that came from deep within me. I know it was the Holy Spirit saying, "Listen, this is important and it is time to act." Maybe the lesson here is to be ready when God says "move" or "listen," and especially to be open to the tough decisions that may need to be made at that point. What followed was an incredible number of puzzle pieces that started falling into place. I want to be careful not to spiritualize the puzzle pieces, but I also don't believe in fate. I do believe that God has a plan for us, and that, for me, now was the time for that plan to be revealed.

His plan might require you to put aside prior judgments and preconceived notions. Things, people or places that aren't the way you are used to or think they should be. One preconceived notion was about network marketing, due to the reputation of some infamous companies. I now understand that this is a legitimate way to market and sell some of the best products out there. The other judgment I naively made, was on Suzanne Somers, whose books I thought were all about her, instead of the important interviews that she has with doctors and scientists. Sorry, Suzanne!

Even being concerned about people's real or perceived perception of you and your life can be subliminally stunting your joy. Are you afraid to be yourself? Are you afraid to be different from what people expect, in a culture of excess and cookie cutter expectations? These perceptions can lead you to say "yes" to too many requests or "no" to many changes that should be made. For me, these were also self-imposed boulders that were also blocking my way.

There may be a big boulder that you need to move before all of the rocks fall into place. Let yourself dream. Sometimes, I think that dreaming may get a bad rap. It doesn't mean that you are not happy with God's blessings in your life, or that you want "more." You may just dream about knowing His purpose for your life, as I longed for. You may dream of having a house, when all you have known are apartments most of your life. I moved 24 times in 43 years. Sixteen times were as an adult, and most of my homes were small apartments. I dreamt of being able to raise my hand when missionaries came to visit, offering a place for them to stay. It grieves me to hear people say that their life circumstances do not allow the pleasure of dreaming. There is a place and a time in everyone's life for realizing dreams. It may not be right this minute, or even this year, gosh, maybe never. But, God willing, just having them in the back of your mind, will enable you to be ready for the opportunities that can put you on the path to realizing them. Listen for the Holy Spirit to tell you when it is the right time. You have the choice to live your life running around in circles or to follow a straight line. The key to the straight line is to first know where you're going.

Since then, I have embarked on one of the best journeys of my life. I went to school, I started a new business, and I wrote a book. I'm eating healthy and feel great with more energy than I've had for years, and I have come into myself again! You can do this too. It's just getting over that hump that propels you into action. When you are on the right path, you will be amazed at what falls into place. If you want to get on the path, this book is for you!

Introduction

Is there such a thing as a Holistic Christian Woman? So often, holistic health and healing are associated with New Age ideas or Eastern Philosophies other than Christianity. It is often connected with people who don't believe in doctors, drugs or surgery. Getting right down to the definition and history of the word takes us back to 1926 when the word was coined as a philosophy.

As a medical term, it is characterized by the treatment of the whole person, taking into account mental and social factors, rather than just the physical symptoms of a disease. The American Holistic Medical Association believes that a spiritual element should also be taken into account. It wasn't until the 1960's that holistic health became known, and has often been referred to as Alternative Medicine.

However, it's anything but alternative! For a couple thousand years, Christians have known that God created man in a holistic way, and for centuries before that, the Jewish people knew it! Just look at how we function. Years ago, when I was living in Portland, Oregon, I visited my grandmother in Washington State. On my way home, there was an ice storm. It took me 5 hours to make the 1 ½ hour drive. I had never been so scared, as my car seemingly had a mind of its own and started sliding sideways going through the mountains. By the time I got home, I was covered in hives. We get stressed and break out in hives. That in itself is a simple enough example of emotions becoming physical. As you'll read in later chapters, putting certain foods into your physical body can create hormonal imbalances that cause depression and Attention Deficit Disorders. The physical becomes emotional.

emotions
physical

For centuries herbs and other plants with their essential oils and other healing properties have been successfully used as medicines. Today, they've gone by the wayside in favor of pharmaceuticals, many of which have these same plant based components added to them! And yet, our society tends to prefer to put their trust in toxic chemicals rather than the natural antidotes. Knowing the time and place for each is one of the keys to optimal health.

> *The dangers of prescription drugs are intrinsic to the drugs themselves, not in how they are administered. No matter how careful the physician in prescribing and how compliant the patient in following doctor's orders, even then deaths and damages occur. In fact, according to the U.S. Centers for Disease Control, more than 100,000 Americans die every year, not from illegal drugs, not from drug overdoses, not from over-the-counter drugs, and not from drug abuses, but from properly prescribed, properly taken prescriptions. In this country, more people die from doctor's prescriptions every ten days than were killed in the 9/11 terrorist attacks.*
>
> *~Dr. David Stewart*
> *The Chemistry of Essential Oils –*
> *God's Love Manifest in Molecules*

We know that there are a lot of things that are in our power to change. We will focus on the positive, and the opportunities that are out there. We will talk about making changes, not only for our own selves and our families, but also how to affect change in our communities, in our schools, and in our hospitals. When we feed the hungry, are we also making them sick? When someone goes to school or enters into a hospital, do they have to be affected negatively by being given food with additives that are linked to diseases? What about our coffee hours and potlucks at church? *or burden ⸬*

As women, we have the unique power of our role in society to initiate the changes that will benefit our children, grandchildren and great-grandchildren. We can ensure the health and well-being of our communities for generations. As women, we can ensure the health and future of our country. It starts with us, but first we need to be open to learning what we can do for ourselves before we can affect the lives of others.

I'm sure you've heard that people surrounded by friends and family are known to live longer healthier lives, and that people who are sick in the hospital have been known to heal quicker if they have a spiritual belief system in place. This is underscored by the enlightening research that has been done on "Blue Zones." It was found that your genes only control 20% of your life expectancy, and that you control the rest with your lifestyle. (Of course we know that God can take us at any time, but this research is based on the physical body.) *Dr. Caroline Leaf*

The Blue Zones include Ikaria, Greece; Sardinia, Italy; Okinawa, Japan; Nicoya, Costa Rica; and Seventh-day Adventists in Loma Linda, California. Dan Buettner, who has been studying these populations for the National Geographic Society, found that the top five Blue Zones may be relatively isolated and scattered around the globe, but they have a lot in common. He is the author of Blue Zones, and he has many programs available through his website that enable people to bring the nine common aspects into their own lives, and the lives of those around them. The nine aspects are:

- They belong to a cultural environment that reinforces healthy lifestyle habits.

- Exercise is a natural part of their day, as in tending their gardens.
- They put family first, from children to seniors.
- They have stress reducing practices built into their lives, of which prayer plays a part.
- They know their purpose and understand their reason for waking up every morning.
- They belong to faith based communities.
- They eat mostly plant based diets and eat meat only sparingly.
- They eat less than they think they need. Many stop when they are 80% full.
- They have a glass of wine with their food.

Other research is turning up that endorse principals like fasting! If you are among the Christians who fast regularly as a part of your prayer life, you may have experienced the side effects of increased energy, better sleep, and the peace that comes after fasting. Yes, science is catching up to all of us who have continued these "primitive" ways of supporting spiritual health and finding that they translate to physical health also.

Holism is on the rise with a fast growing segment of the health industry called Integrative Medicine. Many forward thinking Western medicine doctors are going back to school to get further training on how the body can heal itself if given the chance, and they are finding that it can and does! Health coaches are being trained all over the world. They assess lifestyle, diet, physical activity, spiritual practice, and even career and relationships so that they can facilitate a healing process for their clients.

Women are ready for a change. They are tired of prescription medications, they are tired of not feeling well, and they are just tired of being tired!

The increase of auto-immune diseases, diabetes, obesity, autism, Attention Deficit Disorder (ADD), and the risks being handed down to our children are scary. For the first time in history, the life span of children today will be lower than their parents. It's a full time job sorting through all of the latest studies in health and nutrition which are so often conflicting and not being taken seriously or supported by the average family doctor. It can get depressing when you try to be your own advocate, and it can be very easy to throw in the towel and give up. I urge you to continue to persevere, and if you haven't taken nutrition seriously in the past, please start to do so with this book.

The most important piece of the holistic triad we will be covering is the spiritual dimension. Addressing this area will affect the balance of the other two. Depending on the type of church you go to, you may or may not have a lot of theologically based spiritual camaraderie with other women. In the spiritual realm, yes, there are Bible studies. Some are very theological, others are very basic. Some offer you a chance to delve into yourself as it relates to what you are learning and apply biblical principles, while others are pretty much "information only."

As far as camaraderie, I've found many women's groups tend to focus more on activity - adding to the already hectic, stress filled lives of its members. Baking, fundraising, organizing church activities, and planning for events are all good. However, they attract a certain type of woman who may have a high tolerance for added stress, are master schedulers, or are experiencing guilt over needing to do these things in order to be a good member of her church. The Marys of the church don't always have a support system in place.

Some churches I've belonged to were very social, but the opportunity to be a contributing member of the body was not readily apparent, so most people stayed within their small groups. Sometimes the small groups turned out to be pretty social too, and not as meaningful as they could have been in the area of facilitating and applying Scripture into lives of its members.

This book is for the stressed out Marthas who don't feel the peace associated with the Christian faith. They are so busy supporting their church and doing their part to make it great, that they aren't feeling so great themselves. They are the go-getters who are willing to raise their hand when someone is needed and may have become so over extended they don't have time to care for themselves. May God bless them!

This book is also for the Marys who love their time with God but feel guilty that they aren't in the kitchen or on the committee making things happen. They might also be the shy gal who just blanches at the thought of hitting people up for raffle tickets. They may also be the ones whose prayers in the background are being heard through the noise of busyness. Thanks be to God!

At different times in my life, I have been both and I have felt the pain and the pull on both sides.

The Holistic Christian Woman will attempt to address all of these areas in a balanced way. This book will help women begin to address their health goals by understanding how their bodies work in conjunction with their heart, mind and soul and strength. It is not a substitute for professional medical care, and readers are encouraged to seek their doctor's consent before embarking on something they may be unsure of. It is also just a start. You'll see the theme of stress being addressed in almost every chapter. Stress is one of our biggest enemies, but this book will give you some tools to combat it.

> *"But the fruit of the Spirit is love, joy, peace, long suffering, kindness, goodness, faithfulness, gentleness and self control. Against such there is no law."*
> ~*Galatians 5:22-23*

This is one of my favorite passages, and I suspect it may be so for many people. Who wouldn't want to embody these virtues? Of course God embodies them all, so I guess that's why they sound almost ethereal to me. These virtues are always something always to strive for, as I don't believe you can ever produce enough of any of them. But it is also overwhelming, too, at least for a type A personality like me who puts pressure on myself to achieve goals. I mean, I want to bear all of these fruits all of the time! But in reality, I have good days and bad. Sometimes I feel joy, but I suspect that it isn't the type of joy that Saint Paul was describing. Peace? Yes, I think in 2005... Self-control? Well, you get the idea...

THE FORMAT

We will start with "First Things First," a chapter which sets up a healthy eating plan that can be used while reading this study. It is a practical plan that will get you started, as the logic behind it unfolds throughout the book. Chapters 2-9 focus on each of the fruits mentioned in Galatians, how it is modeled by God Himself, and practical ways that we can see it manifest in our own lives.

In each chapter, after addressing the spiritual and emotional aspect of each fruit, the third leg of our three-legged stool will highlight a physical aspect. It will involve diet, nutrition, exercise, anything that has to do with taking care of the temple that God gave you. It is not only our responsibility, but it is our job to take care of our bodies, so that our choices don't hinder the life and the future that God has planned for us. Do you agree that it will be pretty hard to live out the purpose that God has for us if we are too sick to get out of bed? Too tired to help another person who needs us? Too grouchy to care?

At the end of each chapter there are Challenges and Opportunities. They include questions that make this a personal journey, and they present an opportunity to be held accountable by others. If you are using this book for a small group or a group Bible study, focus on one chapter a week. It may be helpful in enabling you to get the most out of a journey toward a life of peace and joy, with yourself, with others, and with God. I am excited to combine my years of experience as a small group leader with the education that I have received as a holistic health coach. Get out your tool box and make some room for some new tools!

THEOLOGY AND DOCTRINE

The last component I would like to cover before we embark, is one that I feel is always of utmost importance. That is, making sure that whatever you are doing or reading, if there is a spiritual aspect, it is based on biblically solid doctrine. No one wants to read a book, be involved in a study or attend a retreat where they have to be on guard as to what they are learning or experiencing. For that reason, l would like to make sure you are comfortable with my sources.

As mentioned, I am a holistic health coach without any formal theological training. I am an average Christian woman who wants to be healthy, happy and at peace. Around 1973 when I was 13 or so, I understood who Jesus was for the first time. A neighbor had taken my mom and me to a revival of sorts. Not growing up in a religious family, I was, out of the blue, convinced at the deepest level of my being (and at 13 that can be a feat) that Jesus Christ was the Son of God and died on the cross for my sins. As you may be able to relate, it was a roller coaster from there as far as church attendance and attention to this revelation. All of this to say, that when I finally stood up and became attentive around 20 years ago I never looked back. Pastors, priests, small group Bible studies, fellow pilgrims, monks, nuns, books, and years of worship and prayer have provided constant education, guidance, and accountability.

When it comes to the spiritual teaching in this book, I

rely on two sources: Scripture, and the interpretation and teaching taught by the Holy Spirit through the Apostles and their disciples. My personal preference is the New King James Version for Scripture, so you will see that version used as the basis for the quotes.

I've been taught that the interpretation of Scripture, as revealed to the Apostles by the Holy Spirit, is the Truth. Not only in the books that we have in the New Testament, but also what they taught verbally and how they lived physically. As St. Paul wrote to the Thessalonians….

> *"Therefore, brethren, stand fast and hold the traditions which you were taught, whether by word or our epistle."*
> *~2 Thessalonians 2:15*

And also to the Philippians…

> *"The things which you learned and received and heard and saw in me, these things do, and the God of peace will be with you."*
> *~Philippians 4:9*

You will see quotes by many different people. Some you may be familiar with, and some who may be new to you. All gave their lives to Christ, and, I believe, are good examples for all of us, no matter if they went to be with the Lord 2000 years ago or last week.

Depending upon your denomination, you may not be familiar with some of the people I will be quoting, whose lives have been an example of what God can do with us and through us. Some are remembered as Saints, as we are all in Scripture, but with a capitol "S," so that we know we are to examine their remarkable lives, and learn from how God was able to use them despite their sins and transgressions. The author of Hebrews does exactly this in the eleventh chapter as he examines the faith of those who went before him.

To tell you the truth, most of my Christian life, I had not given much thought to the men and women who defended our faith, and kept it growing for 2000 years. I just enjoyed the fruit of their labors. They really fought for God, and in turn, for us! When I think of the fathers of the church, I like to relate them to other "fathers," for instance, the "Father of Mass Production, Henry Ford." Like the naysayers who said that nothing would replace the horse, there were many who said that Jesus could not be the Son of God. Henry Ford plugged along on a quest to convince people, and thankfully, he didn't have to give his life for his convictions. Many of the early men and women who tried to convince people of the Good News did just that. By God's grace, as the Apostles taught, they grew Christianity despite the atheism, agnosticism, and naysayers of their day. The meticulously preserved writings of these Church Fathers have inspired pastors' sermons across all Christian denominations to this day. They inspire me, and I hope they will inspire you by their fruit!

Something else I enjoy and have included to the best of my ability are the Hebrew and Greek versions of the English words. Sometimes it was tough, because there were a few different choices. This is how misconceptions of Scripture begin, so being a purist, I wanted to get as close to the original meaning as I could. During my research, I came across a website called "Hebrew 4 Christians." I was so pleased to find that the author wrote about the Scripture we will be covering, and how he linked it back to our Jewish roots.

Regarding the middot ha-lev (qualities of heart) that are to mark the followers of Yeshua, the Apostle Paul wrote, "the fruit of the Spirit (הָרוּחַפְּרִי) is love, joy, peace; long-suffering, generosity, acts of kindness;

faithfulness, humility, and modesty – against such there is no Torah" (Gal. 5:22-23). Notice that while there is "one fruit" of the Spirit (i.e., "fruit" [καρπὸς] is singular), God produces a manifold yield, just as the Tree of Life (הַחַיִּים עֵץ) produces twelve different kinds of fruit, one for each month of the Jewish year (see Rev. 22:1-2).

Are you ready? Let's dig in!

First Things First

—⁓—

... giving all diligence, add to your faith virtue, to virtue knowledge, to knowledge self-control, to self-control perseverance, to perseverance godliness, to godliness brotherly kindness, and to brotherly kindness love. For if these things are yours and abound, you will be neither barren nor unfruitful in the knowledge of our Lord Jesus Christ.

2 Peter 5:1-8

First Things First

———— ✑ ————

When I found out that I had cancer, I did what a lot of people do. I got on the computer. My shock and the surreal feeling of it all was bathed in tons of information. This became overload, which led to paralysis. I was in the middle of a yearlong certification course to become a holistic health coach. I knew the right things to do to detox my body and set myself up for a bolstered immune system. Why was I glued to the computer reading what I already knew? I guess I felt like I was DOING SOMETHING. As if following my own knowledge wasn't enough.

But what about people who don't have the knowledge? Who haven't heard about radical remissions and studies that have proven that cancer can be avoided and even reversed?

This plan is designed to help people understand that they are empowered to combat their diagnoses. What I needed, and what I think many need, is just a directive. Do this. Trust me. No wordy reasons why, no science behind the scenes with footnotes and a reference guide. Just plain, give it to me straight advice. If you want to go deeper, you can always get back on the computer and try to figure out who is legitimate and trustworthy, and who has the latest scientifically based study. But in the meantime, make sure that you've already implemented as many of my recommendations as you can. Most will be elaborated on throughout the book, and there will be handy reference notes, but in the meantime, just trust me on this. The fact that the body can protect and heal itself if given half a chance is truly one of the miracles that

God has given us.

The interesting thing about this plan is that it not only helps with cancer but other diseases as well. The Center for Disease Control (CDC) estimates that 1.5 trillion of the 2 trillion spent on health care is spent on preventable food related illnesses and disease, and that out of the 79 million people in the U.S. that have prediabetes, nearly 90 percent don't know it!

This is a prevention plan for all diseases and it can turn them around. In fact, not only can it turn around illness and disease, but it can improve energy and sleep. It helps with depression and anxiety and also increases the brain's ability to focus, learn and hold on to memories. This plan strengthens your immune system while it detoxes your body. It also helps regulate hormones. With all of these benefits, it's somewhat of a no-brainer, right? And yet, for many of us it takes finding out that we already have a disease before we take these steps.

When I work with clients one-on-one I take things slowly over several months so that healthy changes can be sustainable. The changes are based on specific issues and goals that are unique to each person, along with their biological abilities to heal and shed weight. That being said, sans your own health coach, if you are the type of person who just wants to lose weight, increase your energy, improve your memory and find joy in life again…

"Food is information. It gives instructions that turn on/off genes, that regulate hormones, and that regulate immune system function. If you put in the right healing foods and take out the foods that are harmful - your body will actually reset very quickly."
~Mark Hyman, M.D.

Just do this and see what happens!

If you've been diagnosed with cancer, diabetes, high blood pressure, fibromyalgia, ADD, or another disease…

Just do this, see how you feel and how your test results change!

Many people have undiagnosed food sensitivities. If you have been wondering if you are one of those people, this will be a good outline to use as an elimination plan. The most common culprits of autoimmune issues are on the "do not eat" list. After the ten week period is over, and you are feeling great, add dairy and wheat back in, one at a time. Make sure there is a weekly interval in between. You may get an "Ah, ha!" moment that will change your life!

It's just 10 weeks. *"A drop in the water bucket of your life."* You can let me know how it goes, in fact, I would love to hear from you! I would also love to know what you think of my attempt to be poetic...hmm...maybe not.

The upshot is, following this guide will put you in a more advantageous position. You *can* take control and be in the driver's seat! Don't let yourself be caught up in the "life happens to me" movement. You are empowered to make changes that will affect your health. Dare I say, God has empowered you through your free will. You will not get this information from your everyday MD. They simply don't have the training or the time, and unfortunately, most don't pay attention to nutritional science. These directives are taken from Functional Medicine Doctors who understand the body holistically, and those on the cutting edge of the most recent studies in their field. While not every one of them will agree with my use of meat, dairy, legumes, fat, etc., I feel that this is a way of eating that can be followed by the average person who is switching out of the Standard American Diet (aka - SAD). You'll see that I've taken out some common allergens. While most people do not have Celiac Disease for example, many people do have a sensitivity to wheat and don't even know it. This may be you! Why not check it out now to see how you feel going off of it for a while? If you have a compromised gut, going on this eating plan will help heal it, and will allow you to process food efficiently once again. A very common condition, called Leaky Gut Syndrome, allows food molecules to pass through the intestinal wall. Your body creates antibodies that go into combat mode to fight off the strangers that were supposed to be contained in the intestines. This leads to a compromised immune system, disease, auto immune disorders, pain, lack of energy, insomnia…all sorts of issues that wreak havoc on your health and happiness. Here is your chance to heal.

> *"Hope has two beautiful daughters; their names are Anger and Courage. Anger at the way things are, and Courage to see that they do not remain as they are."*
> *~Augustine of Hippo*

For many of my international readers, you may be on the right track already! The European Union has outlawed many of the substances that I will be speaking against. Unfortunately, we still have them in America. This is interesting since we source our food from so many of the same manufacturers. They can make them healthier, but Americans don't get them. This is definitely playing a role into the fact that most of the highest ranking "Healthiest Countries in the World" are in the EU and the U.S. doesn't even make the top 20. The last ranking I saw, we were ranked 33rd.

Yet, there is hope in this plan.

So just a brief recap – The latest studies show that diet and lifestyle can prevent up to 95% of diseases, including: Cancer, Cardiovascular, Respiratory, Diabetes, Neurological, and Auto Immune Disorders. These recommendations will get you on the road to a healthier lifestyle. When you embark on this plan, there are a couple things to keep in mind.

WHEN TO BUY ORGANIC

THE DIRTY DOZEN (PLUS) (MOST TOXIC PRODUCE)
1. Apples
2. Strawberries
3. Grapes
4. Celery
5. Peaches
6. Spinach
7. Sweet bell peppers
8. Nectarines (imported)
9. Cucumbers
10. Cherry tomatoes
11. Snap peas (imported)
12. Potatoes
13. Hot peppers
14. Blueberries (domestic)

THE CLEAN FIFTEEN (LEAST TOXIC PRODUCE)
1. Avocados
2. Sweet corn
3. Pineapples
4. Cabbage
5. Sweet peas (frozen)
6. Onions
7. Asparagus
8. Mango
9. Papaya
10. Kiwi
11. Eggplant
12. Grapefruit
13. Cantaloupe (domestic)
14. Cauliflower
15. Sweet potatoes

Source: Environmental Working Group

Everything should be organic and non-GMO. Your body is already straining to fight off the enemy. Help it! Adding more toxins just sidetracks the healing process and reduces your body's ability to fight off the bad guys. I know, buying organic can be expensive. If you cannot afford to buy everything organic, there is a list called "The Dirty Dozen and Clean Fifteen" put out by the Environmental Working Group. When you are working within a budget, it is good to know which produce is known to have the most pesticide residue. I like to use the "Dirty Dozen Plus," which includes two more recent additions.

I would also like to mention what I do when I cannot find a particular organic fruit or vegetable in my small town. Using a ratio of 1:3, mix either apple cider vinegar, or plain white vinegar with water, and soak your produce for about 20 minutes, then rinse. For more delicate items, like berries, keep this solution in a spray bottle, spray them, and rinse. This method can kill 98% of bacteria and remove most pesticide residue.

Something else I would like you to consider: you may feel flu-like symptoms during the first week, along with cravings. This is part of a detoxification process and the cleansing of the harmful microbiome that has been living in your gut. We'll talk more about detoxification and microbiome later. If you stick with the program, these symptoms will pass within a couple days. Also, they must not be taken as a reason to stop the program! As in, "Oh dear, I am coming down with something. I'll wait and start again when I'm well." In fact, I would say that the sicker you feel, the more you need to do this.

Again, it's only for 10 weeks! You can do it! If you are going through this book with a friend or a group, that's great, you have a built-in support system! If you are reading this book on your own, I want to encourage you with these words:

"My children, this is how it is in life. We must set off without waiting for the other to decide. God never calls two or three of us together. He calls each of us personally, at a given time. Woe to us if we do not follow him right away, waiting for a fellow traveler! We miss the unique chance; we miss the right time."
~ *Mother Gavrilia*

I'm guessing that if you're reading this book....it's the right time!

WHAT TO EAT

Half of every plate should be vegetables. Make sure that most are in raw form. The vegetables mentioned below are particularly beneficial. A couple of them are grown below ground, but the focus should be on those grown above ground.

- Cabbage
- Brussel Sprouts
- Onions
- Leeks
- Kale
- Spinach
- Garlic
- Asparagus
- Cauliflower
- Broccoli
- Beets
- Turnips
- Eggplant
- Mushrooms

The other half of your plate should include a combination

of:

- Vegetable Proteins - Beans, Lentils, Peas, Chickpeas
- Animal Proteins - Fish and Shellfish, Lean Meat as a condiment, not as a main course, and Eggs; meat products should be grass-fed, and all animal products should be without hormones or antibiotics; red meat should be limited, and nothing charred
- Fats - Olive Oil, Unrefined Coconut Oil, Flaxseed Oil, Avocados
- Seasonings - Turmeric, Black Pepper, Parsley, Cinnamon, Ginger, Curry, Oregano, Basil, Rosemary, Mint
- Fermented Foods - Sauerkraut and Kimchee (Naturally fermented, not canned)
- Sea Vegetables - Kombu, Nori, Dulse, Wakame, Arame
- Some Fruit, but not as much as Vegetables
- Nuts - Walnuts in particular
- If you have a desire for dessert - One square of Dark Chocolate per day (At least 70% cacao)

Beverages:

- 64 oz of Filtered Water, free of fluoride and chlorine, per day that hasn't come out of a bottle with BPA, add lemon, unsweetened cranberry juice concentrate or ginger root
- 3-6 cups of Green Tea per day, preferably steeped for 6-10 minutes
- Kombucha (Fermented tea)
- Pure Nut Milk

Drink homemade Green Juice once a day and at least one Smoothie. Juicing and smoothies are two of the easiest ways to ensure your raw vegetable intake. Plus, with juicing, the nutrients do not have to pass through a possibly compromised digestive system before they are assimilated into your blood stream. Smoothies ensure that you are also getting fiber with your vegetable goodness. But go easy on the fruit! One piece is usually enough with a few vegetables. Both are necessary for this program. I've found that it is easy to borrow the equipment needed, or purchase them cheap on eBay or Craigslist. Yes, I know, juicing takes time. All of that cleaning up afterwards! I like to look at it this way. Five minutes to clean the juicer or one hour sitting in a doctor's office? Hmm…

WHAT NOT TO EAT

- Gluten (Wheat, Semolina, Spelt, Farina, Faro, Graham, KAMUT®, Rye, Barley, Triticale, Malt in all of its forms, and Brewer's Yeast)
- Sugar
- Bananas, Raisins, Corn, Potatoes (for this program)
- Hydrogenated oils
- Pasteurized Dairy
- Non-organic anything
- GMO anything
- Tap water
- Packaged and processed food (95% of restaurants use)
- Glutamates (Don't worry, I'll talk about these substances in detail in an upcoming chapter)
- Unfermented Soy
- Preservatives (If they are meant to kill bacteria in the food that they're in, they are also killing off the good bacteria in your gut that supports your immune system. Makes sense, right?)

I know that this plan may sound daunting to someone who isn't used to being mindful about what they eat. It could also sound depressing for those who regret the way they've eaten in the past and wish they could go back and do things differently. I've been through both of these scenarios myself. I'm always encouraged by Doctor Hyman's quote, which I mentioned earlier, about the body being able to reset itself if we let it.

What I recommend, is to do the best you can. You can strive for these goals, but you don't need to become a fanatical perfectionist. You may have a family that is resistant to change. In this case, start slowly, and add improvements at a pace that they are comfortable with. Make the modifications for yourself, and offer your healthier options as a way to keep them challenged. There are still millions of toxins attacking our bodies every day through what we breathe and put on our skin. It's actually amazing that, just by paying a little attention, results will come.

"Therefore, whether you eat or drink, or whatever you do, do it all to the glory of God.
~1 Corinthians 10:31

As I've come to understand the sad realities in our world today, I've also come to reason that this is the age that we're living in, and we have to do the best we can. My grandparents lived through a world at war and the Great Depression. Now we live in a world filled with toxins that are attacking our bodies. As people have always done from the beginning of time, we are learning how to survive in our environment, and put our trust in God.

Love

Hebrew
הָבְהָא (Ahabah)

Greek
ἀγάπη (Agapē)

There is no fear in love; but perfect love casts out fear, because fear involves torment. But he who fears has not been made perfect in love.

1 John 4:18

Love

———— ∽ ————

W hen I was 18, I put a bumper sticker on my car. It was the first and last bumper sticker to ever deface one of my vehicles. Yes, I am of the "clean car" bunch. Too bad that doesn't translate to clean from dirt, too. Anyway, the sticker said, "Not Perfect, Just Forgiven."

Even at 18, perfection, and not being held to it, was resonating with me. Knowing that God loved me despite my failings, and that He forgave me, was a huge message that I wanted to embrace. It was also the first time I had been brave about my faith, putting it out there, so to speak. I heard that my dad disapproved. I think it was the first time he even knew about my belief, and it brought back bad memories for him of other imperfect Christians he had been accustomed to in his life. We're all supposed to be perfect aren't we? Others look at us and see our sin, and say to themselves, "And, she calls herself a Christian!"

"In Him we have redemption through His blood, the forgiveness of sins, according to the riches of His grace."
~Ephesians 1:7

How many people run fleeing after visiting Christian churches because they come in and, gasp, see humanity? Hypocrites! "I don't want any part of this!"

But what does Christianity mean? That we're already Saints? Certainly not! It means that we believe in our Lord and God and Savior Jesus Christ, the Son of the Living God who died and rose again. We believe in the Trinity, One in essence and undivided. We believe in the forgiveness of sins, and, yes, in confession and repentance.

What my dad and others may fail to see is the other side of our faith. It's the repentance part. We need to stop trying to be perfect, in every earthly detail, and feeling guilty for not achieving our goals. We need to focus instead on recognizing our sins for what they could be, namely, a learning experience that should drive us deeper into knowing ourselves and understanding what we are capable of. We need to figure out why we do what we do, ask for forgiveness, and repent. Then, accept God's love for us by accepting His forgiveness even when we can't forgive ourselves. This is hard work!

This is the message I needed to understand when I was 18, and I was blessed beyond measure to get it. I don't think I had ever heard the term "unconditional love" until then. A life of guilt over not being perfect, as I define it, no matter how hard I try, can still be a burden, but I have to keep coming back to that bumper sticker. It isn't all about me and what I expect, it's about what God expects of me out of love, and with love.

"A man who has friends must himself be friendly,
But there is a friend who sticks closer than a brother."
~Proverbs 18:24

Have you ever had a friend who is closer than a brother, someone whom you felt loved you unconditionally? I mean an earthly friend. I certainly don't want to stretch Scripture to make it fit my own purpose. The verse may be referring to the Holy Spirit, but I do see a connection, in that God can bring people into our lives who become vessels of His unconditional love.

If we love others the way we are called to love, are we not being a vessel of the Holy Spirit? Is He not calling us to comfort, soothe, guide, teach, and hold each other accountable? I think He is, if it is according to pure intentions and biblical principles. And the true test of a friend who is a vessel of the Holy Spirit is, do they bring us closer to God? Are we refreshed by them? Are we unconditionally loved?

"Now I beg you, brethren, through the Lord Jesus Christ, and through the love of the Spirit, that you strive together with me in prayers to God for me, that I may be delivered from those in Judea who do not believe, and that my service for Jerusalem may be acceptable to the saints, that I may come to you with joy by the will of God, and may be refreshed together with you."

~Romans 15:30-32

"For we have great joy and consolation in your love, because the hearts of the saints have been refreshed by you, brother."

~Philemon 1:7

I have been incredibly blessed with many close friends by whom I feel refreshed. But it wasn't always that way. I did not grow up with friends who were "closer than a brother." In fact, the few I had were more like acquaintances in retrospect. It was no fault of theirs; I just really didn't know how to be in a quality relationship with someone. The type of relationship that leads to mutual growth through love wasn't something I understood until I was entering my 3rd decade of life. God gave me someone who changed my relationships forever.

Her name was Sherry and at this point I don't even know where she is or what she is doing. But for the span of only two years or so, she taught me more about love and friendship than I had ever known was possible. She taught me how to share my feelings and emotions without shame. It was irritating at times. Probing questions were coming at me that I wasn't used to, and I just wanted to run away and hide. But then she would share her own, and finally I learned how to listen to something inside of myself and share in the same way. I even learned how to ask probing, loving questions to go deeper with other people! Together we decided that we both needed to start going to church and reading our Bibles again. We went through feelings of being content, joyful, excited, and scared together. We experienced loss, hardship, arguments, and turbulence. I learned that in true friendship all of these things are temporary, but friendship never fails. I learned that the love of a true friend, like the love of God, is unconditional. And, I learned how to love in the same way. My friendship with Sherry led to knowing how to be a loving authentic friend to others and receive the same friendship back. She was instrumental in setting a course for relationships for the rest of my life, including those with men and ultimately my wonderful husband.

When you think about the friendships in your life, does one person come to mind who has made all the difference? If someone does come to mind, whether you are still in contact or not, perhaps you could drop them a note. An old-fashioned one, a card, with the investment of a stamp, sent snail mail. If I knew where Sherry was today, I would do the same.

Look at your friends today. Do they refresh you, or do they lack a certain authenticity?

"A person should be tried much before being called a friend. You should find out if he has the sense of sacrifice – not towards you, but in general toward all people. If he hasn't, if you see that he is egocentric, preoccupied only with whatever concerns his own self, then you will know that he cannot become a friend. You have certainly noticed that sometimes you may say something like: 'I had such a headache yesterday, I couldn't read a single line the whole day'…and the reply you get is: 'Wait till I tell you what I went

through'... Then he starts talking of what troubles him. He does not care about your headache. He cares only about the things that touch him. This is why he cannot listen to you or anyone else."
~Mother Gavrilia

Obviously, not all friendships will be of the Gold Standard, nor were they meant to be. But I wonder if there is someone in your life who can become a Gold Standard Friend. What would it take to get there? Is there something that you can do on your part? Authenticity is a good measure to start with. Are you really you, and are they really them when you are together? Or, are you acting the part of a friend because you happen to have a sport in common, your kids go to the same school, you are neighbors, etc. There are so many ways in which God brings us together. Keep a watch out for those life enhancing, life changing people He brings our way.

For as the body is one and has many members, but all the members of that one body, being many, are one body, so also is Christ. For by one Spirit we were all baptized into one body—whether Jews or Greeks, whether slaves or free—and have all been made to drink into one Spirit. For in fact the body is not one member but many.
~1 Corinthians 12:12-14

During a recent conference, the speaker mentioned that "Spiritual, Not Religious," is the fastest growing religious identity in North America. You may know people who claim to be part of this same "denomination." What I've found in the people I know who profess this, is that they don't typically belong to a body of like-minded people. They know there is someone or something out there that is a higher power. This may or may not be God, but they know there is something bigger out there. For many, this power may be believed to be inside of them, which means that worshiping in a church is not needed, and usually not wanted. It's interesting that the people I know who profess this as their belief system are some of the most depressed people I know. Many of their lives look fulfilling, but filled with what? I see alcohol and unhealthy eating habits standing in. I see relationships with their friends as anything but unconditional, and family relationships in badly in need of repair and humility. This is against everything Christianity teaches. Many of them are looking to themselves and their own understanding of spirituality as their compass. However, as Christians, we know that the Power is indeed inside of us and it's called the Holy Spirit. Unlike us, the Holy Spirit is infallible, and He calls us to worship as a body and with a family.

"...yes, friendship is the greatest gift from above. That is why He said 'I call you My friends.'"
~Mother Gavrilia

When we are called to love God as He loves us, it includes not only our earthly family, but our heavenly family. Being in relationship with other believers provides an emotional aspect of love, and this is what will happen when you are a member of a church, worshiping, minimally, on a weekly basis, and being an integral part of your church family. This is what the "Spiritual But Not Religious" people are missing. They are missing the sense of love that comes from being in fellowship with others who worship the same God.

I've heard people say that they don't feel the love. They don't feel like they are part of a loving family while they are at church. One of my favorite messages from my priest is about love not being about your feelings, but rather, your actions. He explains that he does not get up every morning to make his wife breakfast with feelings of mushy romance novel type love swelling up in his heart. He does, however, make her breakfast every morning because he loves her. See the difference? It's not about you and your feelings. It's about his wife feeling loved by his actions. He connects this to worship and prayer, and with people who "feel" like they are growing as Christians when their outward life may not reflect it. He connects it to people who have come to him, high on the feeling of being "closer to God." Yet, they are never seen in church, and their family relationships are a mess.

"As Christians we are here to affirm the supreme value of direct sharing, of immediate encounter —not machine to machine, but person to person, face to face."
~Bishop Kallistos Ware

Relational, God centered love, provides a solid platform for emotional health. It involves corporate worship, based on the directives of the Holy Spirit to the Apostles at Pentecost and the church as described in the book of Acts. Without it, the evil one can get a foothold, and the result is that we are not living as God intended. Everything goes out of balance. Love is lost, and loneliness, emptiness, and depression also get a foothold. Loneliness, emptiness, and depression are often soothed in unhealthy ways.

Harvard studied 268 men over the course of 75 years. It was called the Grant Study. They started while the men were in school between the years of 1938-1940 and followed them into their 90's. George Vaillant, the psychiatrist who directed the study during the period between 1972 and 2004, wrote a book called "Triumphs of Experience: The Men of the Harvard Grant Study." It showed that the impact of love and connections with other people, determine our happiness. And it is universal….more so than money or power. His conclusion was that only love is the key to a happy and fulfilling life. He describes two pillars, one pillar is having loving relationships in your life, and the other has to do with fostering ways that don't push it away. A life of joy comes from our connection with others. He said "The more areas in your life where you can make connections, the better." While he doesn't talk about this in a Christian sense, ask yourself, where is the best place for Christians to make connections?

Wow! Don't you love it when studies like this one that cost 20 million dollars (yes!) take us right back to biblical principles? As Christians, we know this, but scientific Harvard studies are good to know so that they can reinforce that God's omnipotent way of creating us as emotionally sound people is relevant in secular society.

A PHYSICAL VIEW OF LOVE

"Therefore I say to you, do not worry about your life, what you will eat or what you will drink; nor about your body, what you will put on. Is not life more than food and the body more than clothing? Look at the birds of the air, for they neither sow nor reap nor gather into barns; yet your heavenly Father feeds them. Are you not of more value than they? Which of you by worrying can add one cubit to his stature?

"So why do you worry about clothing? Consider the lilies of the field, how they grow: they neither toil nor spin; and yet I say to you that even Solomon in all his glory was not arrayed like one of these. Now if God so clothes the grass of the field, which today is, and tomorrow is thrown into the oven, will He not much more clothe you, O you of little faith?

"Therefore do not worry, saying, 'What shall we eat?' or 'What shall we drink?' or 'What shall we wear?' For after all these things the Gentiles seek. For your heavenly Father knows that you need all these things. But seek first the kingdom of God and His righteousness, and all these things shall be added to

you. Therefore do not worry about tomorrow, for to-morrow will worry about its own things. Sufficient for the day is its own trouble."
~Matthew 6:25-34

One of the byproducts of not understanding God's unconditional love for us is worry. If we don't truly internalize that we are being taken care of, through every turn of event in our lives, we worry. If we are worrying, aren't we saying to God that we don't trust His love for us; that things that are happening, or may happen, are outside of His control; that there isn't any BIGGER REASON that we can imagine, even if we don't understand it? I'm sure I don't need to say this, but just in case, the worry about food mentioned in the Scripture above is about having or not having it. God will provide. He is not addressing the quality of the food, i.e.: whether or not to eat MSG, or if genetically modified food is harmful.

Worry creates anxiety and anxiety creates stress.

The Mayo Clinic describes the effect stress has on our body in an easy-to-understand way:

> *"...your hypothalamus, a tiny region at the base of your brain, sets off an alarm system in your body. Through a combination of nerve and hormonal signals, this system prompts your adrenal glands, located atop your kidneys, to release a surge of hormones, including adrenaline and cortisol.*
>
> *"Adrenaline increases your heart rate, elevates your blood pressure and boosts energy supplies. Cortisol, the primary stress hormone, increases sugars (glucose) in the bloodstream, enhances your brain's use of glucose and increases the availability of substances that repair tissues.*
>
> *"Cortisol also curbs functions that would be nonessential or detrimental in a fight-or-flight situation. It alters immune system responses and suppresses the*

digestive system, the reproductive system and growth processes. This complex natural alarm system also communicates with regions of your brain that control mood, motivation and fear."

But we have an antidote! The giving and receiving of love lowers our stress. Studies, like one at the University of Zurich in 2008, which was based on arguing couples, show that the hormone Oxytocin reduces cortisol. We are calmer and more content with more oxytocin in our systems. And how can oxytocin be encouraged? LOVE! Stress is one of our most powerful health hazards, and love is one of our greatest God given stress reducers. As Christians, we don't even have to pull love out of thin air, we are conduits of God's love. We can be vessels that He uses to heal people and prevent disease. Just let that sink in. His power, given to us, makes us so powerful that we can heal people! The "we can heal people" sounds a little woo woo, but hopefully you're following me here! This is a huge responsibility, and I think it's exciting. (As you can see by all of the exclamation points.) Again, we're not talking mushy romance novel feelings here. We are talking about actions which speak louder than words. This is not original I know, but so true.

"Then the righteous will answer Him, saying, 'Lord, when did we see You hungry and feed You, or thirsty and give You drink? When did we see You a stranger and take You in, or naked and clothe You? Or when did we see You sick, or in prison, and come to You?' And the King will answer and say to them, 'Assuredly, I say to you, inasmuch as you did it to one of the least of these My brethren, you did it to Me.'"
~Matthew 25:37-40

One of the time management recommendations that we will be covering later in this book, involves living out your priorities. One of my priorities is to show my love toward others. I need as much oxytocin as I can get!

Each Sunday night when I write out my weekly schedule, I honor the priority of loving others by scheduling it in. I know, this may sound fairly cold and contrived, but I know that weeks of self-absorption can fly by until one day I realize that a friendship has been neglected. The passing of someone I love happens and I regret not letting them know how much they meant to me. So I schedule in quality time with a friend that includes conversation, not just entertainment or shopping. I schedule in writing a personal note to someone I love. I hope you can relate, and that I'm not the only one who has to make an effort when it comes to loving others! I also schedule in acts of love that don't feel like love at the time, for instance, when I do extra cooking for the church pot luck. I have to say, I'm terrible at this, and have groused about it in the past. Is there time to cook for the pot luck? I barely have time to make dinner for the family living under my roof! Hmm... It's an act of love, Cynthia. Be thankful for the people who will be eating your food, that they are in your life and that you are in loving relationship with them as your church family.

"Love is given to us by God. Because God is Love.
The love we give to others is from the Source; it goes
to them and then returns to the Source."
                                        ~Mother Gavrilia

Yes, acts of love precede feelings of love, and feelings of love manifest in acts of love, and as this Divine cycle continues, our stress is reduced. Loving others is also loving God, and at the same time loving ourselves. Oxytocin flying everywhere! Reduced stress can cut off disease and it supports an immune system which can ward off all of those little colds and bouts of flu that we are scourged with throughout the year, not to mention these other symptoms:

- Anxiety
- Depression
- Digestive problems
- Sleep problems
- Weight gain
- Memory and concentration impairment

CHALLENGES AND JOURNALING OPPORTUNITIES

The first opportunity that I would like you to take advantage of, if you don't already, is to start journaling. I know many people say that journaling is not for them. Just for these ten weeks, please do it. After ten weeks, if you don't feel like it helped you in any way, you can abandon it. Journaling is known to reduce stress. It clears your mind and it can bring sense to your thoughts and emotions. It can invigorate and inspire you and it can be proof of growth and accomplishment. My clients are thrilled with the results once they start.

• In your journal, answer the following questions:

> What are the areas of perfection that you hold yourself to, that God may not really care about in the big scheme of things, but are causing you guilt?

> What are the areas of your life that God does care about, and that need to be prayed about, analyzed, prayed about, confessed, prayed about, repented of, prayed about, and prevented from ever happening again?

Here is another way to think about it. Is there anything that you do, or any way that you act, that would drive someone who doesn't understand about sin, forgiveness, confession, and repentance away from God?

How is love being cultivated in your life? Are your relationships where they could be or where they should be? Are there any that you feel you should be more deeply invested in?

- Starting today, in your journal, write down your commitments based on the questions above. They should be written in a way that is positive, measurable, and with a deadline. For example: "Next Monday, I will have exercised for at least 30 minutes each day for 7 days in a row."

- How are you doing with the eating plan? How do you feel? Have you made it through any withdrawal symptoms yet? I really wish I could be there with you, give you a hug, and clean your juicer for you!

Joy

---◆---

Hebrew
הֶוְדָה (Chedvah) or הַחְמֵשׁ (Simchah)

Greek
Χαρά (Chara)

---◆---

Shout joyfully to the Lord, all the earth;
Break forth in song, rejoice, and sing praises.

Psalm 98:4

Joy

———— ෨ ————

"T he ineffable joy of those who love thee..." I hear this in church and always think it sounds so wonderful! Like something I definitely want. I have to confess that I looked up the official definition of ineffable. Even without knowing the meaning, I was pretty sure I hadn't experienced it.

in·ef·fa·ble
inˈefəbəl/
"Too great or extreme to be expressed or
described in words."

Yay, I had experienced it! But fleetingly. For some reason I tend to associate joy with a kid on a roller coaster. After the big drop when the stomach is back where it belongs, the hair is somewhat back in place and a big smile...ah yes...joy! Let's do it again! Or, every Wednesday when I babysit my goddaughters, I open the door, and they rush to hug me. They have even started saying, "I missed you," oh joy! My insides turn to mush just thinking about it! Then there is the joy of knowing you are in the midst of God's will, when everything is falling into place and you just know you were supposed to walk through that initial door, because all of the other doors are opening too, sometimes seemingly by themselves! I love this type of joy. It makes life feel worth living.

First, let's look at the joy mentioned in Galatians 5:22 from a contextual point of view. Saint Paul was writing a letter to a group of churches that he established, and he is instructing them to come back to the grace of Christ.

Some were turning back to the laws of the Old Covenant. Most were confused about whether they needed to continue with or adopt the old laws. Paul is explaining the characteristics of a follower of Christ. Christians are not purposefully doing things or avoiding things in order to receive salvation. They are being led by the Holy Spirit to do or not do certain things. They are bearing fruit that comes from the Holy Spirit in a way that exudes from their inner being and becomes who they are. They don't go to church because they are expected to, or because they feel they should in order to be saved, or because they want to be social. They go because every time the church door is unlocked, it's an opportunity to worship Him. It is what they crave. Worship is their life blood, and there is nowhere else they would rather be. It is their peace, it is their joy. This is the mark of a Believer, someone who trusts in Him and accepts His love and grace without having to work for it, but rather bears the fruit sown in his or her heart, and shares that fruit with others.

The joy that is being referred to in Galatians is not necessarily the emotional joy that we automatically think of. While the emotional joy that is mentioned in Scripture is certainly from God, and is related, this is something on a deeper level that comes out of our very soul, where the Holy Spirit dwells. It is not under our control to produce it, but we can identify and work to control the issues or even sin that blocks it.

Joy can be expressed spiritually, emotionally, or even physically. I believe the holistic woman can experience joy if cultivated. How is that done? Scripture is pretty clear on the topic, and joy is, in fact, mentioned around 50 times! Let's look at some passages and see what they have in common. The book of Psalms has many references.

"But let all those that put their trust in Thee rejoice; let them ever shout for joy, because Thou defendest

them; let them also that love Thy name be joyful in Thee."

~Psalm 5:11

"For You will not leave my soul in Sheol,
nor will You allow Your Holy One to see corruption.
You will show me the path of life; In Your presence is
fullness of joy; At Your right hand are pleasures for-
evermore."

~Psalm 16(17): 10-11

"Be glad in the Lord and rejoice, you righteous; and
shout for joy, all you upright in heart!"

~Psalm 32(33):11

These verses lead us to the main crux of Joy. It is the result of a life lived with God front and center. Trusting Him, loving Him, and being grateful for where you are right at this moment. No worries about the past, no concerns about the future, and knowing that what you are doing right now is good and profitable to your soul and others around you. This is also what Saint Ignatius taught the Ephesians.

"For let us either fear the wrath to come, or let us
love the present joy in the life that now is; and let our
present and true joy be only this, to be found in Christ
Jesus, that we may truly live."

Have you ever felt guilty that you aren't experiencing this Christian joy that has largely been elusive to you? Have you wondered what you are doing wrong? You may be thinking, "I believe in God, that Jesus is His Son and my Lord and Saviour, that He was born, died, and rose for my sake, and so that my sins may be forgiven, and that I may live. I pray, read the Bible, and participate in communion, the Body of Christ. What is wrong with me?" I have found that this requires prayer, and I hope that you also pray about what may be keeping you on the stretcher, like the paralytic by the pool of Bethesda. It may be sin, it may be guilt. It may be that you are waiting for another person to pick you up and take you off. Only Jesus has the authority to say "Your sins are forgiven. Rise and take up your stretcher." Trust in Him who tells you that you can get up and walk.

Are you still on the stretcher? What is keeping you there? What are you waiting for?

I'd like to talk about fear and trust.

What is the worst thing that could happen? Studies have been quoted for years on the biggest fears people have. Public speaking, death, and flying are always at the top. More often on a daily basis I see fears that tend to run peoples' lives and rob them of joy. Some people fear what other people think of them, plus the fear of doing something wrong, which causes them to avoid doing anything at all. Others fear the unknown, "what if the roller coaster breaks down and my car goes flying off into space?" Where does fear come from? Surely not from God! I propose that it comes from thoughts driven by our ego, our pride, and not putting our lives in the hands of God on a daily or even moment by moment basis. You are perfect the way God made you. Trust in His love and protection. Trust in the love that comes through the people that God has put into your life. Trust that you will be taken up to heaven when God says so and not a moment earlier. You can't experience joy if you are always looking around in fear, rather than looking at the potential joy that may be right in front of you.

There is no fear in love; but perfect love casts out fear, because fear involves torment. But he who fears has not been made perfect in love.
~1 John 4:18

Are you living in the moment?

Living in the moment is so tough to do, but it is exactly where joy lies. People who live deliberately with joy, live with little thought about the past, and no worries about the future. Living right now; in the moment. When I'm feeling overwhelmed, I've found it helpful to ask myself, "What does God require of me right now?" It's usually something like paying attention to the person talking to me. Or, eating a sandwich. Not too stressful! There can be joy hiding in an intentional conversation with someone, or in the taste of a sandwich that you actually pay attention to the taste of! This reminds me of the Alcohol Anonymous teaching of living one day at a time to help people addicted to alcohol refrain from drinking. I believe this is a powerful tool for everyone. Thoughts about the past, and worries about the future, rob you of the joy waiting for you today. A technology addiction can rob you of joy; an eating addiction can rob you of joy; a frantic life that involves too many commitments can definitely rob you of joy. We will learn more about each of these in future chapters.

How can we cultivate a thankful heart?

What if I greeted my goddaughters at the door and immediately noticed their muddy shoes? It would start me thinking about how I was going to grab them off of their four little feet before they got mud on the floor, and I would totally miss the feel of their hugs and hear their sweet voices. I may trust in their love for me and may be living in the moment, but instead of a thankful feeling, the focus would be on a negative. Joy is positive. It thrives in thankfulness and gratitude, not in a "glass half empty" world. Thankfulness is the state of mind you are in when you welcome all that God has in store for you.

"For you shall go out with joy, and be led out with peace; the mountains and the hills shall break forth into singing before you, and all the trees of the field shall clap their hands."
~Isaiah 55:12

Whether it is something that you were expecting, weren't expecting, or that He allows in your life to learn from and grow closer to Him. You know that all things work for good for those who love God. You can be thankful for everything. At that point, you become empowered to experience joy. Your initial reaction to opportunities becomes positive, and the negativity, which has been blocking you from experiencing life, begins to take the backseat. Or even gets locked in the trunk!

What are your joy triggers? Often they may be memories, but they may also be very recent and regular.

When we have reached the point of thinking only of our brother and not of our own self, our joy becomes permanent.

~Mother Gavrilia

A PHYSICAL VIEW OF JOY

Joy creates endorphins. Have you noticed how when you feel happy, joyous, or have even just laughed, you feel energized? Endorphins are the "feel good" hormones that mimic morphine and codeine to reduce stress and pain. They modulate appetite, release sex hormones, and enhance your immunity. What's there not to like?

Guess what else creates endorphins. Yep, exercise. Now, before I became a health coach, I knew that exercise was good for me. It's always been included in the triad of wellness. It's been preached and exhorted all over the world by every doctor, magazine, TV ad, and probably your mom. Eat well, exercise, and drink plenty of water. Yada, yada, well, come to find out, the ramifications of not doing these things can be fatal. Not only does the lack of exercise cause you to be out of shape and not look good in clothes, which seems to be the primary concern of a lot of people, but FATAL! Frankly, I'm shocked at the many illnesses can be affected by a 30 minute walk every day. Depression, Obesity, Diabetes, Addiction, Heart Disease, Blood Clots, Arthritis, Cancer, and Alzheimer's to name a few. Just walking! Keeping those lymph nodes in good working order and allowing them to do their job eliminating toxins and waste is huge. I could go on and on about the diseases that can be avoided by the increase in organ function, the energy, creativity and clarity of thinking that will increase, and the quality of sleep that will improve...but I'll spare you...at least in this chapter. For now we are talking about joy, and you will have more of it if you exercise. How is that for simplification?

To underscore the connection between the triad of spiritual, emotional and physical health, an ancient Christian writer, Minucius Felix wrote:

> *"Fortitude is strengthened by infirmities, and calamity is very often the discipline of virtue; in addition, strength both of mind and of body grows sluggish without the exercise of labor. Therefore all your mighty men whom you announce as an example have flourished illustriously by their afflictions."*

From Saint Hilary of Poitier:

> *"The faculties of the human body, if denied their exercise, will lie dormant. The eye without light, natural or artificial, cannot fulfill its duty; the ear will be ignorant of its function unless some voice or sound be heard; the nostrils unconscious of their purpose unless a scent be breathed. Not that the faculty will be absent, because it is never called into use, but that there will be no experience of its existence."*

And Saint Paul's letter to Timothy:

> *"For bodily exercise profiteth little; but godliness is*

*profitable unto all things, having promise of the life
that now is, and of that which is to come."*

~1 Timothy 4:8

How can exercise profit more than just a little, but in all things? We can take Saint Paul's advice to Timothy to pray without ceasing. In this example it would mean linking our spiritual practice with our physical discipline. It's a chapter taken from monasticism that we can incorporate into our own lives. I'm sure you have probably heard of "prayer walking." That's when you go for a walk and have certain prayers that you say, or people that you are committed to pray for. I'm not referring to this as a monastic habit, but I am valuing the time that I spend with God while being in the outdoors, taking in His beauty and remembering others in prayer. This last summer, I found out that "prayer biking" was my thing. It takes it to a whole different level when you have the wind blowing through your hair!

When you hear someone tell you that exercise is good for you, what goes through your mind? Is it positive or negative?

CHALLENGES AND JOURNALING OPPORTUNITIES

- This week, I would like you to identify at least one fear and trust issue that you may have that could be keeping you from experiencing joy. What is it keeping you from doing? Can you do it this week? How will you give this over to the Lord?

- What is one thing that prevents you from being fully present in each task or situation you are in? Do you have an addiction? How can you stop it or let it go?

- I would also like you to pay attention to your responses in the coming week. When you have an opportunity to do something, or a situation presents itself that may have a hurdle, is your first response positive or negative? Now, don't say, "But my concern was legitimate because I was being practical; I'm a practical person!" Nope, sorry, heard it before and I'm not buying it. Pretend your response was like a frown and figure out another way to look at it that would turn that frown upside down! Yes, this is corny, and I know it takes practice for some, but it is beneficial when it comes to changing the quality of your life. Trust me! Be prepared to talk about what you've noticed about yourself next week.

- Are you exercising every day? What specifically are you doing? Make a commitment to increase your activity this week. Jump on a rebounder, play tennis, or walk longer. Start doing something if you don't do anything at all! You can make it fun, play music or go with a friend who supports you. Make it part of your spiritual discipline by listening to C.S. Lewis, homilies, or your favorite Christian podcasts. Pray. This is an aspect of self-care that will pay dividends right away and down the road. If you have not exercised in a while, start slowly, your body will need to adjust in order to reap the benefits of activity.

Peace

———❧———

Hebrew
שָׁלֵם (Shalom)

Greek
εἰρηνεύω (Eiréneuó)

———❧———

*...and the peace of God, which surpasses all understanding,
will guard your hearts and minds through Christ Jesus.*

Philippians 4:7

Peace

———— ✑ ————

I know that you will enjoy what Molly Sabourin has to share about her thoughts on the spiritual and emotional aspects of peace.

P erhaps it is because I am getting older that I feel more vulnerable to various catastrophes; newly emerging wrinkles and aches and pains won't let me forget that years are passing by with alarming speed, and four decades of life experience have stripped the rose-colored tint off the lens through which I view this chaotic world. Upon waking each morning, my mind is flooded with possibilities, the majority of them ranging from unpleasant to nightmarish, unfortunately:

- Forgotten appointments
- Financial struggles
- Missed deadlines
- Ebola
- Relational conflict
- Cancer
- Lost library books
- ISIS
- Wasted time/energy/money
- Freak accidents
- Entovirus D68
- Adolescent angst

I'm not a grim person, honest – just an aware one. I can't listen to the news or log onto the Internet without being reminded in a thousand different ways of how much evil, stress and illness is pouring down upon our lives. And what makes it weirder is that these hellish stories are intermixed with celebrity gossip and beauty tips. It's crazy and unpredictable out there.

And yet, in spite of it all, I believe with all my heart that serenity, love, beauty and goodness are accessible at any time, in any circumstance. They must be sought

Make me to awaken daily with a willingness / to roll out readily, accompanied / by grateful smirk, a giddy joy, / the idiot's undying expectation, / despite the evidence.
~ *Scott Cairns, The Idiot Psalms*

after of course, and we must sacrifice quite a bit to acquire these heavenly attributes, but if we are willing to put in the effort, then authentic, eternal joy can and will override our tendencies toward fear and despair.

Recognizing that each of us is unique in terms of our weaknesses, strengths and backgrounds, I do not assume to know what coping methods would work best for you when it comes to finding peace in the midst of chaos but for what it's worth, I will share some of mine. May God bless us all with a sustained desire for what is good and profitable for our souls, and the strength to release that which keeps us shackled to earthly cares.

1. There is such a thing as being "too informed"

Web MD, CNN, My Yahoo Homepage: these are all things I have grounded myself from due to their propensity for working me into a no good, hysterical frenzy. You know those waves the apostle Peter ogled at, when he was attempting to walk on water, instead of continuing to look at Christ? That's what news and medical sites are to me. The moment I start fixating, all wide-eyed and slack-jawed, on their up to the minute updates, gruesome details and doomsday-ish predictions, I start drowning. It is not naive to protect your brain and heart from an onslaught of sensationalist journalism, only prudent . A "well-informed" yet paralyzed with fear Molly Sabourin is no good to anyone, my precious family most certainly included.

2. Live in the moment, with Thanksgiving

I am absolutely convinced that present tense living and gratitude are the keys to all peace, all wisdom, all joy. The following piece from "Life Transfigured: A Journal of Orthodox Nuns," nails it!

> *"If we as Christians truly believe that our lives are lived under the sign of the Cross and in the light of eternity, then we must believe that God is with us in all the changing fortunes of our days. And we must also believe that despite natural disasters and human ills, evil is not finally triumphant and death is not victorious. In our lives there are no chance events, no irrational twists of empty fate, but rather the ever-present workings of a provident God, Who uses all means to lead us into the harbor of Christ.*
>
> *"When we begin to feel, however faintly, the truth of this, we shall find much to be grateful for. The spirit of thankfulness is a necessary part of the spiritual discipline of living in the present moment – with God – and not in the past or the future. We cannot know what will happen tomorrow, or even tonight; we cannot change what is already past. But we can be grateful today for the blessings of today – the blessing of life itself, the blessing of communion with God through prayer and the Holy Eucharist, the blessing of repentance, the healing of forgiveness. Even the small, seemingly trivial, moments in our day – the sight of a bird in the sky, the greening of a tree, the laugh of a child, the voice of a friend – speak to us of God if only we wish to hear, for everything of beauty,*

of light, of love, comes to us from Him.

"In such small moments, as much as in the dramatic crises of our lives, the headlong rush of time opens upon eternity. If we learn to live quietly, attentively, faithfully, in the "now" which alone truly exists for us, we shall be prepared by degrees for the "everlasting now" which awaits us after death. If we do not find and follow Christ in the present moment, we shall not recognize Him at the end of time.

"Let us ask of God a grateful heart, and let us resolve to give thanks each day for the day itself and the presence of Christ in it, sustaining our life by His hand and giving courage to our struggles, zeal to our repentance, contrition to our prayer, and stability to our labors. If only we will make an effort, we will find that giving thanks to God — even in adversity — opens our hearts to see blessings we had not thought to find."

3. Go offline, and be Kind and Helpful to the people in my local community

Let's face it, an excessive amount of social media can incite anxiety, judgey-ness, jealousy, insecurity and terrible unproductivity. Everything in moderation, right? See the problem, or my problem anyway, with Facebook and such is that it reduces whole flesh and blood individuals into mere holders of opinions on hot-button political, social, moral and Theological issues. If we agree with those opinions, they are our "friends," if we do not, a chasm grows between us that becomes too hard to cross via 40 character rebuttals to their opposing positions. Relating to our "neighbor" in this way falls way short of Christ's commandments to love, serve, turn the other cheek, etc. These on-line "relationships" are agitating instead of salvific, and discouraging instead of hopeful.

Investing in my community, however, allows me to

work with, volunteer with, laugh with, and generally interact with my neighbor as a human being, as opposed to a faceless opinion. By going out of my way to find beauty in that person right in front of me, focusing on where we can connect, and by actively attempting to encourage that person in whatever big or small way I can (a warm smile, a kind word, a listening ear, a helping hand), divine joy spreads virally, and bridges are formed. Stepping outside of myself to uplift someone else always, always brings me peace.

> *"Stand at the brink of the abyss of despair, and when you see that you cannot bear it anymore, draw back a little and have a cup of tea."*
> ~Elder Sophrony of Essex

4. Surrender my expectations

The quickest way for me to get frustrated and irritable is by holding tight to my own assumptions about what would be "best" for me. See, if I had my own way, I'd never be hurt, or stretched, or humbled, or uncomfortable; my patience would not be tried nor my faith tested. My default desire is ease and gratification, which are temporarily thrilling, but not exactly character building. I lack the will power to choose salvation over self-preservation all on my own.

Many, many, many of my best laid plans have been thwarted, and I will admit I did not always handle the disappointment with grace and dignity. In hindsight, however, I can see exactly how those blows to my pride and presumptions were necessary for my spiritual growth, and for my ability to empathize with the struggles of others. As hard and sometimes scary as it is to surrender my longings and expectations to Christ, praying "Thy Will Be Done" with fear and trembling, the letting go brings with it a new realization of how omnipresent God's compassion is. Viewing whatever befalls me as an opportunity to become ever more long-suffering and merciful allows me to rise-above the fear of failure, interruption or being disdained. Peace is trusting Christ to provide not what I want but what I need, because He loves me.

O Lord, I do not know what to ask of You. You alone know what are my true needs. You love me more than I myself know how to love. Help me to see my real needs which are concealed from me. I do not dare to ask either for a cross or for consolation. I can only wait on You. My heart is open to You. Visit and help me, for the sake of Your great mercy. Strike me and heal me; cast me down and raise me up. I worship in silence Your holy will and Your unsearchable ways. I offer myself as a sacrifice to You. I have no other desire than to fulfill Your will. Teach me to pray. Pray You Yourself in me. Amen.

~Metropolitan Philaret of Moscow

5. Pursue beauty

And finally, there is beauty – the kind of beauty that brings me to repentance and inspires me to keep on keeping on believing in Light that cannot be extinguished by worldly darkness. True beauty quiets the noise causing my eyes to be blinded and ears deafened to all that is good, noble, and pure. I find it in nature, in music, in literature, and most especially in the hymns, sacraments, and services of the Orthodox Christian Church. I've grown more cautious of what I allow to penetrate my fragile being. When I open my mind to depravity, titillation, and materialism, they tend to take root and make me feel, well…just plain yucky and dissettled. True beauty is medicinal – very healing.

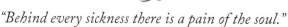

"Behind every sickness there is a pain of the soul."
~Mother Gavrilia

A PHYSICAL VIEW OF PEACE

Happy is the man who finds wisdom,
And the man who gains understanding.
~*Proverbs 3:13*

Do any of you feel guilty that sometimes all you can think about is cookies? I went through a donut phase about a year ago. I never ever, except maybe once a year, have a donut. But all of a sudden, I found myself stopping at donut shops and putting away a couple before even leaving the parking lot. Jelly or chocolate? Why decide when they are so affordable? Might as well throw in a lemon filled too. This feels like confession, so even if you guys have no idea what I'm talking about, and can't relate, I'm feeling much better!

Looking back, I suppose that there were about five minutes of pleasure, but I know it was followed by a yucky feeling in the pit of my stomach, in my heart, and in my brain. I had to get to the bottom of this. I had to get to the big WHY behind the binges. If I didn't, my future would be grim. If you can relate to this, it's not too late!

> *"Being addicted to sugar and flour is not an emotional eating disorder. It's a biological disorder, driven by hormones and neurotransmitters that fuel sugar and carb cravings — leading to uncontrolled overeating. It's the reason nearly 70 percent of Americans and 40 percent of kids are overweight."*
> ~*Mark Hyman, M.D.*

Not only can you undo the damage, but you can also turn genes off and on with diet and lifestyle. If you think that you are stuck with diabetes or other diseases because they "run in your family" you couldn't be more mistaken. Dr. Walter Willett, along with a group of Harvard colleagues, reported in The New England Journal of Medicine, that 91 percent of all Type 2 diabetes cases could be prevented and reversed through changes in lifestyle and diet. The key to success is to catch it early, but even catching it late can turn your life around for the better.

Your mother was right, there are consequences to everything that you do. Insulin spikes and resistance, caused by sugar and other simple carbs, rob you of peace. The crash afterwards, along with the regret and the fear that you are on the road to lying in a hospital wondering, "Why did God let this happen to me?" robs you of your peace and challenges your faith.

I could go on all day telling you about the effects of sugar and carbs on your body. How glucose levels and insulin resistance compromise your gut bacteria, your immune system, encourages fat to pile on, and drives you to distraction with hormonal imbalances. But I'm not. We're going to talk about the brain, "your brain on drugs," to quote an old TV commercial.

Dr. Frank Lipman calls sugar the "available without prescription drug." We are dealing with a worldwide drug addiction that most people think is acceptable.

> *"Addiction is a condition that results when a person ingests a substance or engages in an activity that can be pleasurable but the continued use/act of which becomes compulsive and interferes with ordinary life responsibilities, such as work, relationships, or health."*
>
> *~Psychology Today*

Did you know that sugar is eight times more addictive than cocaine? Dr. Pamela Peeke, author of The Hunger Fix, cites a study that concludes, *"refined sugar is more addictive than cocaine, heroin or morphine."* (As an aside, anything that comes in a yellow, blue, pink....I don't care what color...packet, is DOUBLE TABOO. So, don't even think about it! These refined substances may taste like sugar, but they are linked to cancer and are known to stall weight loss. The little packets of powder look even more like cocaine than sugar does, if you ask me.)

If you are like me, the number of people you know with dementia and Alzheimer's has been growing. People who have cancer, diabetes and autoimmune issues have also been growing. If you think one of the connections may be to sugar, you're right! Dr. Mark Hyman cites a study where 600,000 products were analyzed and 80% of them turned up to have added sugar. These products are killing us by feeding our addiction without us even knowing it.

There are two people that I like to reference when speaking about neurological disorders and nutrition. One is Dr. David Perlmutter. You may know him as the author of *Grain Brain*. Along with his conclusive studies on grain, Dr. Perlmutter's research also tells us that sugar and carbohydrates affect your memory, and worse, lead to Alzheimer's. He calls them "The Brain's Silent Killers." Those senior moments that we all have, like walking into a room and forgetting why? He says that it's the start of more to come, and it's preventable!

As we know, sugar and carbohydrates are linked to diabetes, so it's no surprise that diabetics are more prone to dementia and Alzheimer's. In fact, having diabetes doubles your risk for Alzheimer's disease. As if that wasn't enough, the diabetes connection is twofold, and also gets back to the damage that is done to our bodies through pharmaceuticals. A study published in the Archives of Internal Medicine shows that women given statins for high cholesterol have a 44% increased risk for becoming a Type 2 diabetic. This means that you are statins, and are not diabetic, but are eating a diet high in sugar and carbohydrates; you are at great risk for developing both diseases as you age. Since diabetes and high cholesterol are preventable and even reversible, you can prevent this from happening.

I remember a year ago when I started feeling like I was getting to be a "scatterbrain," and was appalled that I seemed to be falling into the "ditsy" category at times. Not that I have anything against ditsy scatterbrain types, I just knew that it wasn't me. I wasn't functioning at my best, and this symptom was a sign that my brain was not working as well as it used to. This also coincided with a period of time when I was turning to eating one or two scones a day as comfort food. Ah, this all makes sense now! I was killing my brain with my idea of comfort. Once I did a "reset" and cleaned up diet, my focus and memory improved.

By bringing our souls to life as women, God entrusts us with the great responsibility to make the right decisions when it comes to the health of other people. As women, we are still the main caregivers today from a global perspective. Women tend to control the meals that are eaten and the schedules that are kept, which to a large extent are the main components of a healthy life. Scheduling and meal planning become the foundations of health which manifest physically, mentally, emotionally and spiritually. Women ensure the health of future generations and ultimately the health of our countries. If things continue as they are though, we're doomed.

When we consider how sugar and carbs are messing with an adult brain, just think of what they are doing to kids. There has never been a time when more children have been diagnosed with learning disabilities, Attention Deficit Hyperactivity Disorder (ADHD), and autism. Between the glutamate created excitotoxins in our food, and the sugar slipped into almost everything, children's brains are being stunted. And what if a child also has an undiagnosed gluten sensitivity? We haven't talked about gluten/gliaden/glucosophates and the effect they can have on the brain, but even without getting into wheat studies, the end result is that you can imagine how many children are on pharmaceuticals who don't need to be.

The number of children who are smart but are perceived differently because of what they are being fed is a crime. I urge people to look into the nutritional factors behind perceived learning disabilities before putting a child, or yourself for that matter, on pharmaceuticals that can create further damage. After cleaning up your diet, you can outline your real symptoms to the doctor, not fake symptoms based on poor nutrition.

Now please don't get up in arms thinking that I am against all drugs. I do know that there is a time and place for pharmaceuticals. However, in this case, there are just too many studies about the effects of poor nutrition connected to learning and behavioral disabilities to ignore the facts.

My other favorite source for how food affects the brain is Dr. Daniel Amen. Dr. Amen is a psychiatrist and brain disorder specialist. He is a bestselling author eight times over, and together with Pastor Rick Warren, Dr. Mark Hyman, and Dr. Mehmet Oz, is one of the chief architects of "The Daniel Plan," which is a successful diet and lifestyle program aimed at getting healthy together as a church family.

One of his books is called *The Healing ADD Power Program*, and in it he explains four ways ADD devastates children and adults if left untreated.

- 35% never finish high school.
- 52% have substance abuse problems.
- There is a higher incidence of divorce, incarceration, job failure, and financial failure.
- There is a higher incidence of obesity, diabetes, and Alzheimer's disease.

Next time, before you put something sugary in your mouth, say to yourself, "nothing good comes from sugar," not for the guilt factor, but from the stand point of positioning yourself to fight back. I want you to lay this foundation in your memory. If you are like me, you grew up in a culture that sells sugary cereals for breakfast as health food. You were probably raised to think that cans of beans and peas are good for you, so you buy without looking at the label. START READING LABELS TODAY! Not the front, that's for marketing. Not Nutrition Facts, those numbers are easily manipulated and can mean nothing... that includes calories. But rather, the **Ingredient List**. If it has added sugar, or any other sweetener, don't buy it. If it has an ingredient you aren't sure about, don't buy it.

When you see the word "sugar," I'm estimating that 90% of the time, it's not even pure cane sugar, its genetically modified beet sugar, because it is the cheapest. Several years ago, I found out through allergy tests that my body had an adverse reaction to beet sugar, and so I started reading labels. It was enlightening to say the least! Now I'm wondering if the reaction was the actual beets, or the GMO ramifications of ingesting more chemicals. Either way, I stopped eating beet sugar for 4 months, (along with a few other culprits) and the chronic pain in my neck and shoulders went away.

I hear you saying, "I get it, but I'm in the trap and can't get out! I have cravings, and I am so tired and emotionally spent from life in general, that I'm having trouble even thinking about saying no." Is that what you were saying? Well, that's why everyone is talking about cleansing.

A cleanse can be a highly effective tool for detoxification. It also resets the way you eat, gets rid of cravings, balances your microbiome and strengthens your immune system. They are very hot right now. But as with anything that's hot and trendy, you need to be aware of danger signs. Those short skirts that are hot and trendy? You're in your 60's? Danger, danger! Some cleanses are too radical, and if your health is already compromised, you may be putting your body under too much stress. I personally prefer a few medically supervised programs for some people. Biotics Research is one that I have experience with and recommend. Another one I like to use is the "Clean" program by Dr. Alejandro Junger. At first, I was scared when I found out that it was the one that Gwyneth Paltrow raves about. I typically run and hide when programs are endorsed by movie star types, but this one proved to be worthy of the endorsement. Of course, your health coach can also personalize one for you based on your unique needs.

A proper cleanse eliminates toxins from your diet, and gives your organs a rest so that they can begin to function normally again. It bolsters your immune system and creates energy through pure and simple (read God-given) foods. The results can be incredible! More energy and better sleep are a given due to the biological shift in our gut, but joy, peace, and all of the ways we are called to walk on our Christian path, come more easily too, because our minds are clearer and our hormones stop getting in our way. We can process emotions again, and our prayer becomes more focused as our brain starts functioning smoothly again.

"Acquire a peaceful spirit, and around you thousands will be saved."

~*St Seraphim of Sarov*

CHALLENGES AND JOURNALING
OPPORTUNITIES

- If you are attempting to stick with the eating guidelines set forth in the first chapter, how are you doing? Do you think that a cleanse will help? Read "Clean" by Dr. Alejandro Junger. It will go into more detail than I have gone into here, and then decide if it is for you. Consider seeking professional guidance.

- Take the partial list of hidden sugars on the next page to the grocery store, or go through your pantry to see if you're getting more than you think.

- Looking at Molly Sabourin's examples, what are some ways that you are going to bring peace into your life this coming week? Make a list in your journal and choose one to focus on in the coming week.

NAMES OF ADDED SUGARS

- Agave Nectar
- Honey
- Barley Malt Syrup
- Invert sugar
- Beet Sugar
- Lactose
- Brown Rice Syrup
- Maltodextrin
- Brown Sugar
- Malt syrup
- Cane Crystals (or, even better, "cane juice crystals")
- Maltose
- Cane Sugar
- Maple syrup
- Coconut Sugar, or Coconut Palm Sugar
- Molasses
- Corn sweetener
- Palm Sugar
- Corn syrup, or corn syrup solids
- Raw sugar
- Dehydrated Cane Juice
- Rice Syrup
- Dextrin
- Saccharose
- Dextrose
- Sorghum or sorghum syrup
- Evaporated Cane Juice
- Sucrose
- Fructose
- Syrup
- Fruit juice concentrate
- Treacle
- Glucose
- Turbinado Sugar
- High-fructose corn syrup
- Xylose

Longsuffering

---⌇---

Hebrew
וְחַנּ (Channun) (Gracious)
or
רא מי‚(erekh apayim) (Long of Nose...
meaning Slow to Anger)

Greek
Μακροθυμία (Makrothymia) (Great Sacrifice)

---⌇---

Therefore seeing we also are surrounded with so great a
cloud of witnesses, let us lay aside every weight, and the sin
which does so easily ensnare us, and let us run with patience
the race that is set before us.

Hebrews 12:1

Longsuffering

Elise Adams brings us wisdom on the topic of longsuffering, and I am so grateful that she is sharing her journey with us.

Suffering is not a topic any of us warm to easily. The idea of slogging through difficulty that feels endless and horrible just doesn't sound uplifting. In fact, I've wondered why Paul included longsuffering in this list of "gifts of the spirit." If this is one of the ways God's Holy Spirit pours into us, I'm not sure I want a part of these so-called gifts.

At first glance I thought that maybe my life qualified me for this "longsuffering" gift of the Spirit right out of the gate. When I list out all the "tough stuff" I've been through from childhood abuse, addictions, abusive relationships, homelessness, and years of poverty it seems there has already been plenty of suffering to go around.

Even if you don't have my laundry list I'm quite sure you've suffered enough as well, haven't you? We can all list the trials and tribulations we've been through. At least, we imagine we've suffered enough. Can't God just find a different gift to bless us with?

"By your patience possess your souls."
~Luke 21:19

What I want to know, however, is what does God intend for me with this gift of His Spirit? Is this longsuffering Paul describes in this list of the gifts of God's Spirit, all about going through terribly tough times or something else entirely?

When I took a closer look at this verse I was shocked, quickly realizing that what I'd always thought about this particular gift came from a completely wrong perspective.

Now, I'm no theologian, but after searching for all the references to this word in the Bible (turns out there are 17 of them) I discovered that "longsuffering" is actually an adjective, an attribute, often ascribed to God Himself. This word doesn't refer to Jesus Christ sufferings for us while here on earth either. Instead, this attribute is used to describe how God puts up with us, His wandering, silly, tripping-over-ourselves children.

That's when I discovered something that has me falling in love with this gift! The International Standard Bible Encyclopedia says that in Hebrew this word literally means "long in the nose" or "long in breathing." Longsuffering is all about taking a deep breath, about endurance. And patience.

"I understood that there is much more to wonder at, to rescue and to love in the ruins of man than in the most magnificent ruins of stone.... Courage, faith, patience, endurance and, above all, hope and joy can take root and blossom in the human heart, if it is given Opportunity, if it is given Love."

~Mother Gavrilia

These days I relate deeply to this attribute of God's character in a whole new way and I long to exemplify this Divine Patience in my own life. As a child I saw a lot of impatience and even anger in my home. My parents struggled with a legacy of domestic violence and alcoholism from their own broken childhoods. As I look back now it seems that I spent every night cowering on the staircase hoping my dad wouldn't hit my mom and praying my mom would stop yelling at my dad. I'm sure it wasn't literally every night, but that memory of anger, impatience and fury has stuck with me my entire life.

As an adult the struggle to contain my own fury at injustice, victimization, and poverty has often overflowed uncontrollably on those around me. In fact, I lost my first two marriages due to my own anger. In reaction, I swallowed and stuffed that anger for the next four years, falling into a relationship where the person I was with inflicted his anger on me, but after years of dishing it out, I figured I deserved it.

Now, after all that "surviving" my own outbursts and living through other' ranting, raving anger, I have a particular impatience with my own impatience! How can I continue to spew out my own feelings so harmfully? How could I allow someone else to hurt my small children and me during those years of abuse and homelessness? How do I now move past those days of out-of-control fury, outbursts, and vindictiveness?

The only way I know is to take one step at a time into the gift of God's miraculous longsuffering. I find it deeply ironic that this gift is described in a way that confuses us, in the English language anyway. For those of you who share my struggle with impatience and anger, doesn't holding our tongue often feel particularly miserable? To keep that misery inside, to allow God to handle any retribution and revenge required in the situation instead of taking things into our own hands, does require a type of temporary internal suffering.

I know that my Heavenly Father has no desire to leave me there, twisting in the wind of my own impatience. He's shown me incredible patience, allowing me to learn at my unreasonably slow human pace, while calling me to show myself and those around me the "great kindness" and "plenteous mercy" He gives me so freely.

"Peace I leave with you; my peace I give you. I do not give to you as the world gives. Do not let your hearts be troubled and do not be afraid."
~John 14:27

How can I refuse to pass along the same love He's shown me? How can I turn up my nose (pun intended) when He's offering me the benefits of being "slow to anger," of "long patience," and of having His Perfect Peace?

On an internal, experiential level, this aspect of God's love the Bible calls "longsuffering" has immediate and emotional value for me. When the definition of longsuffering outlines its opposite as "quick to anger" and the "quick-breathing anxiousness" that comes with retribution, revenge, and a judgmental spirit, the payoffs for accepting the gift of longsuffering become even clearer.

The temporary discomfort of holding my tongue, refusing to spew forth short tempered, anxious reactions, gives way quickly to the gift of God's indescribable peace. It is the repeated experience of giving way in the Presence of His Peace that heals those broken, angry places in my heart. The greater gift hidden behind this seemingly ugly word is that this gift of God's Holy Spirit is one of the antidotes for my attempts to assuage my anxiety, anger, and selfishness on my own.

Have you read the verses directly preceding this seminal "Gifts of the Spirit" litany? Paul lays out how those who participate in drunkenness, hatred and strife won't enter the Kingdom of God. I don't know about you but when I'm struggling with anger or hatred I am miserable! My emotions are riled up and in a state of panic. Believe me, I have wasted years in such anxiety and anger.

Yet, God doesn't call me to "pull myself up by my own bootstraps" or to "get over it kid!" No! He hands me the free gift of longsuffering. He says to me, "I will give you MY peace, MY longsuffering patience, MY kindness and love, gentleness and meekness in place of your anxiety and anger!"

I wish I could declare to you today that I never experience out-of-control anger any longer. The truth is much uglier. Experiencing a God-led marriage where I must daily and weekly humble myself to make amends for my ugly moments has led to a level of freedom from my own habits in a way I used to believe was impossible, however. The experience of slowing down my reactions, taking a looooong breath, allowing God's Spirit to enter into those silly daily conflicts has made all the difference. Where I once had no self-control, today I have a moment to choose—a Divine "way of escape" as Promised in His word. This has opened up a whole new world of possibility.

Today I am not enslaved to short-tempered reactions or impatient and angry outbursts. I am not completely free of all such reactions, but I do know I have the Gift of God's Spirit in me ready to pour forth a Divine reaction instead. And strangely enough these same spiritual benefits of God's blessing of longsuffering carry right into the physical benefits....in my life all these areas are truly interconnected in a Divine whole-woman experience of freedom and grace.

A PHYSICAL VIEW OF LONGSUFFERING

There have been many studies done in the disciplines of biology, medicine and psychology on the dangerous side effects of stress. The other day, however, I came across a TED Talk by Kelly McGonigal on making stress our friend. She contends that stress can remind us how beautifully our bodies have been created, how we're made to endure with grace and strength the difficulties that come against us. Kelly went on to outline several landmark studies showing that when people *believe* that stress makes us stronger stress has no negative effects on our bodies whatsoever. In fact, stress occurring to people who believe that it won't harm or damage them actually physically strengthens them! Stress for these people acts like exercise for our cardiac and neurological systems!

Not only does longsuffering offer me the opportunity to involve myself directly in the flow of God's unlimited love for me and those around me, but it offers me the ability to believe differently about the injustices and injuries I endure in life. Changing what I believe isn't a simple snap-of-the-fingers process, I know. Truth has to be written on my heart in a deeper way than a simple intellectual understanding for it to take root deeply enough to change my physical condition. When we talk about attitude and faith so many of us just roll our eyes! How can I really believe differently about stress? How can I just start believing I am "fearfully and wonderfully made" when I'm in constant pain from chronic fibromyalgia or waking up in a dead fog from depression every morning? When I have no energy, when I struggle to think, how can I work on knowing God cares for me enough to break through this despair?

For me, the hope is found in the simple fact that long-suffering is a *gift* of God's Holy Spirit. I am not required to drum up enough patience to breathe deeply, slow down my heart rate, and participate in a calm, peaceful demeanor. What I'm asked to do here is accept the gift and walk in it, accepting that longsuffering is available to me for the asking, then practice its reality in my life. The benefits to my health literally, figuratively, and spiritually are enormous!

This is never truer than in those moments when anger and impatience threaten to overtake me. I've often described the waves of anger as a powerful force of intense, furious energy waiting to sweep me away into insanity! This sense of being out of control, desperate, and panicked by my own emotions carries directly into tense, aching muscles and long-lasting chronic pain. In

...so that we ourselves boast of you among the churches of God for your patience and faith in all your persecutions and tribulations that you endure.
~2 Thessalonians 1:4

fact, I connect my experience of physically disabling pain, brain fog, and depression to my struggle to "let go and let God" handle my life instead of trying constantly to battle through it on my own.

The gift of longsuffering promised in this list is deeply

comforting and literally pain, stress, and struggle reliev-ing. When I accept the gift of slow-breathing, long-last-ing patience for myself as well as for those around me, pain and depression ease.

After nearly two decades of disabling pain that iron-ically went hand-in-hand with decades of out of control anger, there is a whole-person peace that exists in me today that literally wasn't there in my 20's or for most of my 30's. Earlier I mentioned that I'm not a magically never-angry-again person and that is certainly true. Yet the constraint strain of holding back an unending tide of anger has eased. Practicing accepting God's peace in place of that strained and constant sense of injustice and bitterness has had dramatic physical benefits.

What I've experienced as I slowly yet consistently practice turning over all my internal ugly places to Christ, is nothing short of a deeply rooted restoration of my spirit in line with His Spirit. This has led to a very literal healing of the physical damage those early experiences of abuse had caused. I spent my 20's locked in sleepless-ness, intense chronic pain, headaches, a desperate hunger (both physical and spiritual) as well as seemingly endless attempts to "fix it" myself.

I tried pharmaceutical drugs, including psychotro-pic medications for depression, anxiety and panic only to find myself addicted to tranquilizers and struggling with addiction. I tried sleeping for a couple years, only to end up in even more pain and depression. I tried physical therapy with some success only to run out of insurance. I tried all sorts of supplements, exercises, essential oils and home remedies—all to some success yet nothing "stuck," the pain always came back. It was not until I accepted the fact that the root of my physical pain was spiritual and emotional distress,that I began to experience free-dom and healing.

Sometimes when I share this nuts-n-bolts side of my recovery from anger, bitterness, and being unforgiving it sounds pat, like I'm offering a "just fix your insides and your outsides will be happier" type of solution. The only confidence I have is in the fact that this solution is sourced by the Holy Spirit and not any answers I've come up with myself. When it comes to longsuffering the ancient answers are truly the most modern.

The practices of longsuffering, the baby steps to great patience and peace, are all about invoking the only true Source of Peace available to me. When I reach for prayer instead of impatience, I have reconnected my spirit to His Spirit directly. Why wouldn't I expect that the gift of longsuffering would then flow into my spiritual, emotional, and physical life? As I outline some of those practical "let's practice" steps, please remember that without the Source of Life, any step we take is pointless. Let's take Him at His word, let's prove these ancient practices in our daily lives and live in the complete, whole, new life we've all been offered!

"Everything in this world happens either because God wills it or because God permits it. As far as I am concerned, whatever gives me joy is by God's will. For God is all merciful and all good. And just because He is all merciful and all good, he also permits some things that are necessary for the perfection of my soul. These things may be most unpleasant to me, but then, how can coal be transformed into a diamond?"
~Mother Gavrilia

Challenges and Journaling Opportunities

- Meditate on the context of longsuffering shared in this chapter. What has patience meant to you in the past? What might patience, being slow to anger, longsuffering, kindness, and God's love mean to you as you go forward? Can you accept His gift of Perfect Peace?

- Can you relate to Elise Adam's exploration of the roots of her anger, outbursts, and impatience, what emotions rose to the surface for you? Choose a safe place and time to journal, or speak to a trusted friend about these feelings. How might you release some old, historical beliefs about your emotions and allow the light of God's longsuffering-kindness to overtake them and transform them?

- Having released some bitterness and accepted God's peace emotionally and spiritually, how might you release some angry tension physically? Elise has shared that she's found great healing physically after releasing her need to stay angry and offended. How can you walk this reality out in your physical life? Swing your arms out wide, take some extra deep breaths, and breathe in the gift of oxygen! That BREATH is evidence of God's gift of longsuffering, literally translated long-breath into our physical lives!

Kindness

❦

Hebrew
שָׂחָן רָזב וֺנָח רֵסָע (Chesed)
or
תוּבִידָנ (Nedivut) (Generosity)

Greek
Χάρις (Charis) or χρηστότης (chrēstotēs)

❦

*I have been crucified with Christ; it is no longer I who live,
but Christ lives in me; and the life which I now live in the
flesh I live by faith in the Son of God, who loved me and
gave Himself for me.*

Galatians 2:20

Kindness

———— ❧ ————

When I think of kindness and God, at first, the two were hard to connect. Not because God isn't kind, it's just that kindness seems like a trite word when it comes to someone as big as He is. "Oh thank you, that was very kind of you." If you are like me, you see that lovingkindness is so closely related to goodness, peace, and gentleness, that they mesh together like a finely woven fabric. Often they are so close to each other that they seem interchangeable at times. There is a reason for this. When you go back to the original Hebrew text, the word used is "hesed" or "chesed." As Scripture continued to go through translations, translators have struggled with the word, because it really doesn't have an exact match in other languages. The Greek translators of the Septuagint, as far back as three centuries before Christ, used "eleos" which is similar to mercy or pity. The Latins used "misericordia" or mercy and compassion. Luther used the word "gnade," or grace, as the closest he could come to a German equivalent. But then it all becomes clear when you find that the word we use most often is "kindness" and was shortened from two words that were originally used by Myles Coverdale who completed the first English version of the old and new testaments in 1535. The words were "Lovingkindness."

My deduction, and often the deduction of the translators, is that, what sets kindness apart is that it involves an action or words that evoke emotion. When someone is kind to you, you feel loved, grateful, and perhaps a sense of warmth. When you are kind to others, these same feelings come back to you. And, I have found that if you have fostered peace, goodness, and gentleness in your life, kindness flows out of you, just as it flowed out of God. It flows out of love. It all comes together, holistically, if you will.

In the Old Testament, we see God's kindness flourish as He tried to open the eyes of His people. Manna rained down from heaven, rain came, waters parted, and a host of other acts that are too numerous to mention. God loved the world and His actions showed it.

But the best was yet to come.

> *"Because of His great love for us, God, who is rich in mercy, made us alive with Christ even when we were dead in transgressions - it is by grace you have been saved. And God raised us up with Christ and seated us with Him in the heavenly realms in Christ Jesus, in order that in the coming ages He might show the incomparable riches of His grace, expressed in His kindness to us in Christ Jesus."*
> *~Ephesians 2:4-7*

Our Lord and Savior Jesus Christ was God's ultimate gift of "chesed." He practiced a form of kindness that went beyond anyone's definition of the word, when He showed it to all people equally. It didn't matter about their station in life, their gender, their age. It didn't matter if they were one of God's chosen people or not. And it certainly didn't matter if they were known sinners! He not only spoke in kindness, but His acts of kindness went beyond the earthly stamina given to the human body. Remember how we talked about love being an action in our first chapter? His compassion moved Him to turning His love into actions.

I was having dinner with someone several years ago who professed to be an atheist. He was challenging me to accept that charity and kindness were acts of selfishness. Because doing nice things for other people makes us feel good, we do them for our own benefit. It has nothing to do with Christianity or any other faith. My dinner partner thought that Christians do acts of charity merely because we are being exhorted to do so through Scripture.

I wish I could have put into words what I can now. (I have the irritating habit of getting all confused when confronted and not being able to say anything that makes sense.) Where is he now? I would say....Exactly! And those feelings that we have come from God in order that we might be propelled to do more of whatever it is that makes us feel good! Charity follows His tenant to love each other. It comes from love and God is love. Our warm feelings are given to us by God! He created these feelings in us. That's what sets us apart from other mammals. The Big Bang didn't give us warmth of heart after feeding the poor.

It's like the process of making babies, being fruitful and multiplying. It feels good, so we want to do it. Everything that feels good, that feels right, that feels satisfying is from God, *if it glorifies Him at the same time.* And acts of kindness, of lovingkindness, do exactly that!

Kindness is about refusing to live in darkness. Kindness is accepting the light of Christ and His goodness, and extending the same to others around us, and around the world.

"When you see a person, any person, make yourself nonexistent, really, as an entity, and enter into that person's soul, even if he is a wrongdoer or someone you do not understand. You must do this! For he, too, has in him the breath of God, the spark of Christ; and a heart that beats like yours. In other words, you yourself are reflected in him. Unless you do that, you cannot help the other person. And what is then the purpose of loving only God, of raising her hands, vertically, to the Lord and not extending our arms,

also horizontally, to take in the whole of humanity, if possible, and so turn our body into the sign of the cross."

~Mother Gavrilia

———————————⁓———————————

Kindness began when Eve ate the apple, and God didn't turn the entire board game upside down. And now kindness has run amok. People who don't even know God are doing it. Random acts of kindness are everywhere! Even people who believe that they are no more important, or just as important in this world as trees, ants, and dogs (yes, nutrition school opened my mind to things that went way beyond heath) are practicing the God given desire to be kind, without even knowing it. Finally, here is one epidemic that we can be grateful for! Even television commercials are using examples of kindness to sell things, and Facebook posts are sharing evidence of it to spread warm, fuzzy feelings. I love watching the Holy Spirit work in and around unsuspecting people!

But it isn't all warm and fuzzy. There is sin, and where sin lives, kindness does not enter. When I first moved to the town where I live, I started checking out all of the churches to find one that I would attend for week day services. I knew that I would still continue to drive to Chicago each Sunday to stay with my current parish family. The first church I went to had pews, which just didn't seem Orthodox enough to me at the time. I also didn't like that the icon of St. John the Baptist wasn't on the iconostasis next to Christ where

"And you shall love the Lord your God with all your heart, with all your soul, with all your mind, and with all your strength. This is the first commandment. And the second, like it, is this: 'You shall love your neighbor as yourself. There is no other commandment greater than these."

~Mark 12:30-31

he "should" be. I wrote the church off. The second one was empty. The only ones in attendance were priest, and I believe, the priest's wife. Another was too big and too "Greeky," to quote someone close to me. I like to sing along with the service, and while I can sing in Greek, I just like to know what I'm singing, word for word, since it is also a form of prayer. Oh, how I am cringing with embarrassment while I share this with you! How prideful! How lacking in everything that "Charis" means! Will this stay in the book or will I chicken out? We will see. Lord have mercy.

"Remember, O Lord, Your tender mercies and Your lovingkindnesses, For they are from of old. Do not remember the sins of my youth, nor my transgressions; According to Your mercy remember me, For Your goodness' sake, O Lord."
Psalm 25:6-7

The church I ended up choosing was the closest I could come to my standards, which were very high as you've noticed. (More cringing.) The people and the priest were, and are still, wonderful. However, I think that I knew I was on the brink of needing to find one church to be fully present in, rather than dividing myself up between two. There were some traditions that I was missing during my local worship, and I wanted them to be a part of my life. So after seven years, I ended up at the first church I had checked out and dismissed. It taught me a lot about kindness. First, there was the kindness of all of the people in all of these parishes who were nothing but kind to me. I never felt like I was being judged in any of them. And then, I eventually understood the lack of my own kindness, all in the name of "discernment." Being kind extends into our prideful judgment of people, places, and things. Turn the sword of Scripture on yourself, Cynthia. Forgive me everyone.

Can you relate to my pain? Have any of you ever done this? Have you walked into a church where people were worshiping, and because you didn't understand the way they were doing it, immediately judged them as being wrong? I did this within my own denomination, and as we all know, there is a lot of this going on cross denominationally. You drive by churches that you wouldn't dream of going into and you see a lot of cars. These people put God first by getting out of bed, going to church, and are worshiping Him in the way that they understand worship. Perhaps their way is not perfect, but perhaps your way is not perfect either. But either way, God is being praised, and people are being loved in brotherly fellowship together.

Learn from my mistakes. Don't spiritualize judging by calling it "discernment."

Kindness of heart – Lovingkindness – Charis – involves purity of heart. It thinks the best until proven wrong. Kindness must extend toward our sisters who worship differently from us. Are they clapping and singing and jumping up and down? Are they standing with serious faces under head coverings? Do they love God with all of their heart, mind, and soul, and strength, and their neighbors as themselves? Do they know that Jesus died on the cross for their sins and was resurrected?

"For God so loved the world that He gave His only begotten Son, that whoever believes in Him should not perish but have everlasting life."

~John 3:16

A PHYSICAL VIEW OF KINDNESS

Have you ever been lonely and felt like eating a pint of ice cream while watching TV? Have you ever been stressed at work and all you can think about is getting home to a glass of wine? When one or more areas of our life are out of balance, food, drink, and unhealthy forms of relaxation can call out to us. If we respond in unhealthy ways, the energy is sapped from us, and so often what we think will make us feel better, actually makes us feel worse.

Basic knowledge of self and being able to inspect our lives for "bubbles and dents," as I like to call them, is the key to getting a handle on where we need to make changes. Where are you experiencing a bubble? Too much of something, out of proportion with the rest of your life, may be keeping you from experiencing life to its fullest. How about dents? These would be areas in your life that are lacking, which lead you to try to fill the emptiness with something else not so healthy.

So, let's talk about showing lovingkindness to ourselves, especially when it comes to cravings and a lack of discipline. As already mentioned when we talked about sugar, cravings can be associated with a deficiency our body has. Too many people beat themselves up about their cravings instead of looking at the root cause. Cravings are not a weakness but an important message from our body. Cravings may mean that you need to take out a couple foods, and they will go away. They also may mean that you perhaps need to add in a couple healthy foods. They may mean that it is summer and you miss the days of going out for ice cream with your dad. They may also mean that the nutrients you are putting in are not substantial enough, or even that there is a void in another area of your life that you are filling with food.

As you can see, there are some very real, behind the scenes, reasons for cravings. They can be emotional, nutritional, or chemical, conscious or subconscious. Kindness to yourself includes introspection and getting help when you need it to figure it out.

Does this resonate with you? Do you feel like it's your fault when you can't stick to a diet? That you are weak and not disciplined? Take heart with knowing that many food-like substances today are actually created to create an addiction. Genetically modified foods are often referred to as "Frankenfoods." I like to extend the definition to foods that have had toxins added in order to make them tasty and addictive. I know. If you work for a food manufacturer, I apologize.

> *"The foods we are eating now...if prepackaged...are specifically created to create an addictive response. And studies show that sugar is eight times more addictive than cocaine!"*
>
> *~Mark Hyman, M.D.*

The quote above explains why there is sugar added to almost everything! The founder of The Institute For Integrative Nutrition, Joshua Rosenthal, states,

> *"The part of us that cannot be controlled is actually our inner guide to health and happiness. This innate wisdom is always trying to make us feel better by urging us to eat foods that will dissipate, at least temporarily, our physical tension, give us more energy and lift our moods."*

We need to trust ourselves and learn to listen. Why not start the practice today to listen to what your body needs? If it is a type of food, let yourself eat something that answers the call, but here is the important part... Answer the call with what God put on this earth for us. Could Jesus have eaten it 2000 years ago? Then it's OK. If it has been "man-handled" with chemicals added and ingredients you can't pronounce, then leave it alone and find something pure. This will put you on the road to health, healing, and peace.

While I was in school, wading through 100 dietary theories, I kept waiting for one that recommended ice cream, at which point, I was going to run out and buy some Talenti Sea Salt Caramel Gelato. I mean, we kept hearing conflicting reports on meat, dairy, grains, etc. There had to be SOMEONE who had scientific evidence that dairy mixed with sugar had a redeeming quality. However, sea vegetables kept coming up! This brings up another craving, salt. (This is my lead in to seaweed.)

Now that I've lost you, seriously, sea vegetables are the bomb! (I have never used that expression in my life, just FYI). Sea vegetables are one of the most nutrient- packed foods on earth. They reduce cholesterol, improve digestion, counteract obesity, strengthen bones and teeth, and contain antibiotic properties. They are also purported to make you more beautiful (I think that's an improved skin reference.) And, if, here is the big tie in, if you crave salt, due to their mineral content, they will curb your cravings for salty things. Yes, my potato chip friends!

If you are like me, you are wondering what in the world qualifies as a sea vegetable since they sound so yummy, and you are finding your car keys right now to run out and buy some. I am here to help! If you are not surrounded by high quality grocery stores, you may need to find a health food store or Asian food store, then, just Google some recipes, and you'll be shocked by the secret sea vegetable culture you'll find online!

SEA VEGETABLES

- Arame - Semi sweet. It's a great side dish and yummy with buckwheat. (As if buckwheat could get any yummier!)
- Hijiki - Black, robust and also a side dish.
- Korbu - Light flavor, chewy, tenderizes food and helps with digesting beans. It helps create wonderful stocks and soups.
- Nori - Tastes similar to tuna. Use as a sushi wrap or get flakes and use as a condiment.
- Dulse - Savory, delish when roasted with seeds.
- Wakame - Sweet, lovely with carrots, parsnips and legumes.

CHALLENGES AND JOURNALING OPPORTUNITIES

- This week I challenge you to buy a sea vegetable and get back to your group, or even drop me a note on my website.

  What did you buy?
  How did you fix it?
  Did your family like it?
  Would you make it again?
  Do you feel more beautiful?

- Do an individual study, and then talk with your group about the differences between judging and discernment. Make notes in your journal about situations you've been in, and whether they've required one or the other.

Goodness

⸎

Hebrew
בוט (Tub) (Chesed)

Greek
ἀγαθωσύνη (Agathōsynē)

⸎

And we know that all things work together for good to those who love God, to those who are the called according to His purpose.

Romans 8:28

Goodness

---ॐ---

Goodness started at the dawn of creation and came from God. When He created light, it was good; when He created Heaven, it was good; when He created the earth and the seas, it was good; plants, the seasons, day and night, it was all good. We need only to look out the window to see that we live in shear goodness, and I haven't even covered half of it from the first chapter of Genesis. We also know that God created Eve because it was not good for Adam to be alone. He provided everything that they needed, not only to survive, but thrive. The Old Testament is filled with God's goodness to His people, and to other God fearing nations around them. Jumping ahead to the New Testament we are blessed with God's coming in the flesh as an act of goodness to save our souls through the person of His Son Jesus Christ. When His Son departed, He once again, in His goodness, gave us His Holy Spirit, which first came down upon the apostles, and then into us through baptism. We know God's goodness extended into giving Himself to us, to live in us for eternity. As Christians, to do anything but good is contrary to the foundation of who we are. Sin is what we call the opposite of goodness.

Goodness comes from our soul's reaction to people and circumstances, and manifests itself as love. We are to listen to God in us and imitate Him.

But are we true to God who is in us? And therefore, are we true to ourselves? We are made pure through baptism and accepting His Holy Spirit to dwell in us, but what does it mean if we continue to defile ourselves, and therefore suppress His goodness?

"If I refrain from doing something bad, it is because I do not want to sadden God. Not because I fear him, but because I love him. I am neither God's captive, nor have I surrendered as is done in a war. I want to offer myself every day, willingly, lovingly, now that I am alive, today, and not just be an obedient corpse. . . . I could do it the other way too, but then I would be a lifeless body."

~Mother Gavrilia

Just as goodness started at the dawn of creation, I propose that it also starts with each of us at the dawn of each day. After acknowledging the goodness of God in our morning worship, it is cultivated in our souls and in our actions throughout the day. Each day creates memories. Everything we do, everything we hear, everything we are exposed to, affects who we are. The memories build on the foundation of God dwelling within us.

Knowing that God is within us comes with a responsibility, and it is not to be taken for granted. His goodness comes in many forms, from what He provides us, what He teaches us, and what He allows us to do.

Imagine a little girl who is so loved by her father that he gives her a little money to go down the street, meet up with a friend, and go to dinner. He trusts her to do the right things, and closes the door, feeling love and so happy that he could do this for her. She goes down the street, and instead of going to Sarah's house, she decides to go to Pam's, someone her dad doesn't feel is a good influence on her. They go to the candy store, then to a movie that she knows her dad wouldn't approve of, leaving them nothing for dinner. She ends up coming home hungry, with memories of impure content instilled in her soul.

Does God show His mercies to us when we squander

His gifts? We know that He gave us all of the money and material possessions we have. Are we responding with thanksgiving or do we take what we have for granted?

God's goodness is about His goodness to His people, and our goodness to others, but also, our goodness to ourselves. Are we being good to ourselves when we eat food that He didn't create, and that causes us harm? Are we doing good to ourselves when we overeat and over-indulge in good food? Are we doing good to ourselves when we fill our minds with content that isn't edifying?

"We are who we are through our memories.

"Great is the power of memory, a fearful thing, a deep and boundless manifoldness; and this thing is the mind, and this I am myself. What am I then? What is my nature? A life various and manifold, and exceeding immense. Look, the plains and caves and caverns of my memory are innumerable and in-numerably full of innumerable kinds of things, either through images, as all bodies; or by actual presence, as in knowledge of the arts; or by certain notions or impressions, as the emotions and feelings of the mind which—even when the mind does not feel—the memory retains. And whatever is in the memory is also in the mind—over all these different memories I run or I fly: I dive into memories on this side and on that, reaching as far as I can, and there is no end to them. So great is the force of memory, so great the force of life, even in the mortal life of man."
~St Augustine the Confessor, Confessions 10

"Surely goodness and mercy shall follow me all the days of my life, and I shall dwell in the house of the Lord forever."
~Psalm 23:6

Carefully cultivating your experiences and memories can promote goodness. "Let it gooooo, Let it gooooo!" Yes, I'm singing that song from Frozen. I can't help it. The phrase "Let it go" will never be the same for me. This is a memory I want to keep for the rest of my life: one of our goddaughters at four years old, running around our living room dramatically singing at the top of their lungs.

I know that many of my friends think that I'm odd and don't understand what the big deal is. I watch extremely little TV. I don't go to movies. And I tend to only watch movies on TV that were made prior to 1940. What? Yes, this really makes me an outsider. I can barely keep up with cocktail conversation. Justin who? What does he do? That movie that won five academy awards seven years ago? No idea. I'm a real wet blanket.

I find that what passes for entertainment in our culture is not about goodness and doesn't promote it…in fact it leads us away from it. I'm all about protecting my soul and my memories. Sexual humor and content can bring thoughts out of my memory and into my consciousness that aren't edifying. Crass words and humor just make life cheaper for me, and I want to live a high quality life. Reading books and watching TV shows geared toward 12-year-old boys (yes, this is the demographic those sitcoms are written for) are just a waste of time when you consider all of the

"Therefore, having these promises, beloved, let us cleanse ourselves from every defilement of flesh and spirit, perfecting holiness in the fear of God."

~2 Corinthians 7:1

really high quality stuff out there. I've heard people say that they wish they had time for the high quality stuff, and at the same time, they're up on all of the current movies and TV shows. Sigh. The one that is tough for me personally is language. If I am at someone else's house and end up seeing a recent movie or TV show that includes supposedly socially accepted language, it can slip out of my mouth a month later and can never be taken back. I know I'm a minority here, but hopefully there is someone reading this book who can identify with having a standard of living that rejects the decline of popular culture. What's wrong with proper? What's wrong with class? Why does the world we live in today seem to value the lowest denominator more than the highest?

Toxic content creates toxic memories that are contrary to goodness and go against Paul's admonition in Philippians.

> "Finally, brethren, whatever things are true, whatever things are noble, whatever things are just, whatever things are pure, whatever things are lovely, whatever things are of good report, if there is any virtue and if there is anything praiseworthy—meditate on these things."
>
> ~Philippians 4:8

Memories have a way of coming out of nowhere to affect our focus on goodness as God intended. They can lift you up certainly, but they can also bring you down. Careful curation of life experiences ensures long term health, spiritual, emotional and physical.

Yes, I did say physical! Even your physical health is affected. For example, the strain that your body undergoes when overcome with regret or shame about something is very real. Your body releases cortisol and affects your adrenal glands, triggering other stress chemicals like adrenaline. Also, cytokines, which are pro-inflammatory, increase. We know inflammation and stress are bad for our bodies and promote disease. We know that adrenal glands can be overworked until they give out, and we know that high cortisol levels can cause weight gain, and specifically, yes, muffin tops.

A PHYSICAL VIEW OF GOODNESS

As I mentioned in the previous chapter, a good rule of thumb, is to be careful about eating anything that wasn't eaten in biblical times. Or, that Jesus wouldn't have eaten, or something along those lines. Some people use our grandparents in this example, but that no longer holds true. Grandparents today may have been brought up in the 50's which was the start of the major decline of quality food.

Detoxing and cleansing are real buzzwords these days. But it's more than a fad, it's a necessity that we need to pay attention to and incorporate into our lives. Once used only for people who abuse drugs and alcohol, the term "detox" now encompasses helping our over taxed body rid itself of all of the junk that makes its way into it. The intruders come from what we put in our mouths, what we breathe and what we put on our skin. They come in the form of substances that can mimic hormones, overload our livers and cause brain dysfunction. I heard Dr. Mark Hyman mention that the average baby has 287 known toxins found in their umbilical cord before they even take their first breath. Toxic chemicals that were not intended by God to be in a baby....or anyone for that matter.

What is food? I propose to you the controversial opinion that its purpose is to sustain life. Eating it the way God intended tastes good, but you wouldn't think so from looking into the average grocery cart. One day while standing in line, I was thinking about the Israelites. God rained down manna from heaven. I wonder how many said, "Ooooh...yuck....manna. Not manna again! I won't eat it, it needs lemon." This is often the response I get when people talk about vegetables.

One way to start healing is by doing what you are already doing by now, reading labels. We touched on this when we talked about sugar, but there is so much more to consider when it comes to discerning God's goodness in our food.

As mentioned before, but worth mentioning again, I don't mean the part that says "Organic," "Healthy," "Gluten Free," "Low Fat," "Low Sugar," or "Part of a Heart Healthy Diet" on the front. That would be called marketing. The front of the label is geared toward people who believe that the product is good for them if it has these words on it. That is not you! In fact, in the health food section you'll find some of the most convoluted ingredients added to products to make up for what has been left out. I also don't mean the back of the label marked "Nutrition Facts," which includes calories. This information, including worrying about calories, is old school, and meant for people who used to believe that these numbers mattered. Yes, many doctors and even old school dieticians and nutritionists will still tell you that these numbers are important. They aren't. The way the numbers are manipulated to make things look like they should, based on the latest dieting hype, means that they cannot be trusted. Have you ever seen a can of spray oil that says fat free? I think they all do. Makes ya think, doesn't it?

One day I invited some friends over for lunch and a movie. Well, not exactly a movie, more like a documentary. It was on grocery shopping by Jeff Novick. If you are lucky enough to have a friend who is a health coach, you too could be invited over to watch videos on how to read food labels! And if that wasn't enough, we ate quinoa salad and chocolate pudding made with avocados and bananas. I know, you all want to be my friend now.

Seriously though, this video is great. It's called "Should I Eat That?" He is funny and engaging. I use his techniques plus some others I've learned, to do grocery store tours and pantry overhauls with my clients. I highly recommend that you get a copy of this DVD and have a house party of your own!

Something serious that I want you to be on the lookout for, are added glutamates. Notice I said "added," just like I refer to "added sugar." Our body needs and uses glutamates and sugar. However, we don't need to consciously add them in. Our body has it taken care of. This is part of God's great plan. He has it all covered! Our body needs certain nutrients and enzymes, and it extracts them from natural foods that are consumed. When food manufacturers throw in more to make pre-packaged and processed foods tasty, it makes us sick. They can get away with it, because the FDA deems these additives "safe." They are, in the way that we are supposed to get them, in pure, clean food. But now, their overuse is causing us harm.

"And out of the ground the Lord God made every tree grow that is pleasant to the sight and good for food. The tree of life was also in the midst of the garden, and the tree of the knowledge of good and evil."

~Genesis 2:9

Glutamates are neurotransmitters normally involved in learning and memory. It's also an excitatory neurotransmitter, which means it stimulates areas in the brain and other parts of the nervous system. In some cases, it can be an excitotoxin. Excitotoxins appear to cause nerve-cell death. This is linked to Alzheimer's, but also people with fibromyalgia are found to have abnormally high levels of glutamate their brains. Glutamates in the brain affect all of the senses, cause anxiety, impair motor skills, and create and enhance cravings. This leads to eating disorders and addiction. You may want to refer back to "Sugar and Peace of Mind" which also connects excitotoxins to ADD. Hence the glutamate red flags.

Do you remember the fervor against monosodium glutamate, aka, MSG? There have been numerous studies on MSG and we now know that it is harmful. It creates leptin resistance in the brain which causes overeating and weight gain. MSG is an excitotoxin, meaning that it over stimulates the brain causing the production of excessive amounts of dopamine. This creates a drug-like rush that provides a brief sensation of wellbeing, which of course, would be highly addictive. In the process, brain cells are destroyed. While many people swear that they do not eat MSG, little do they know, they are still getting other hidden forms of what can only be viewed as the same poison. For a more in-depth examination of MSG's impact on your health, take a look at Dr. Russell Blaylock's excellent book *Excitotoxins – The Taste That Kills.*

When we talk about women's hormones being out of whack, emotions out of control, and no willpower, do you see now why you are being set up to fail by the very foods we have thought are good for us? This is another case of knowledge being power when it comes to improving your health.

A PARTIAL LIST OF GLUTAMATE RED FLAGS ADDED TO OUR FOOD

- monopotassium glutamate
- glutamic acid
- hydrolyzed vegetable protein
- hydrolyzed plant protein
- autolyzed plant protein
- autolyzed yeast
- sodium caseinate
- calcium caseinate
- modified corn starch
- textured protein
- yeast extract
- yeast food or nutrient
- soy protein isolate or extract
- natural flavors
- natural ingredients
- maltodextrin
- citric acid
- carageenan
- some dough conditioners
- malted barley
- malted barley flour

Challenges and Journaling Opportunities

- Are there memories in your life that make you cringe? How can you release these and let them go? Are there memories waiting to happen, that you may need to consider guarding yourself, or protecting your children against?

- Make a copy of the glutamate list and look in your own cupboards, or take it to the grocery store next time you go shopping. I apologize in advance for the depressed state that you will be in. You'll need a nice long walk with some "happy" music when you've finished.

- How are you feeling? If you've been staying true to the eating plan, I suspect that you feel great at this point! Keep it up! If you don't feel great, this week's information on labeling may help clean out some toxins that are still lurking in your foods. Are you eating out at restaurants or other people's homes? I'm sorry to say that you are still consuming toxins if this is the case. Try to make sure you are eating only home cooked meals, at least for a couple of weeks!

Faithfulness

———— ∽ ————

Hebrew
וְאֹ֫מֶן (Omen)
or
תּוּנָמֶאֱנ (ne'emunut)

Greek
Πίστις (pistis)

———— ∽ ————

I was glad when they said to me,
"Let us go into the house of the Lord."

Psalm 122(123):1

Faithfulness

————— ∽ —————

Giving is where it's at. Not getting. You're thinking, thanks, Cynthia; this was worth the price of the book! I know we know that. We hear it all of the time. But stick with me for a bit.

When I think of faithfulness, I like to think of the ways that we show our faithfulness to God. His faithfulness to us surrounds us daily when He continues to bless us, no matter how much we don't deserve it. Worship is one of the main ways that we show our faithfulness to Him. As Christians, it may seem like a no-brainer, but how many times do you hear people say that they don't go to church because they don't get anything out of it? They didn't feel "fed." They were left flat, so why go?

"O come, let us sing for joy to the Lord; Let us shout joyfully to the rock of our salvation. Let us come before His presence with thanksgiving; Let us shout joyfully to Him with psalms. For the Lord is a great God, and a great King above all gods."
~Psalm 95(96):1-3

First, what is worship? It is the act of giving love, and all the reverence and adoration that is due to God alone. As faithful servants, we worship. In some churches some of the services are called "Liturgies," which literally means "the work of the people." It's work to worship! We are so used to multitasking and giving and receiving information at Internet speed, that to slow down and concentrate is a feat!

In many churches there is contemporary singing, listening to music and sermons, watching dramas, dance, and even then minds wander from the focus on God and worshiping Him.

I just want to say, folks, that being there isn't about what you are getting. Worship is an action that comes from you and starts in your heart. And yet it is still a small fraction of what happens when you go to church. We are so used to being consumers that we walk into churches and decide whether the worship there is worth buying or not. If we walk in from a judgmental perspective to decide if the church is worthy of us and our time, we are definitely going to see the bad! And there will always be less than optimum things that Satan will put right in front of our very noses. Now, I know I sound preachy, but if you read the previous chapters, you know that I'm preaching to myself. I'm not pointing fingers at others and ignoring the plank in my own eye. Rather, I think discussion on this matter is good and enlightening for us all.

When you walk into a church that you are not familiar with, how do you feel? What are your thoughts? Are there preconceived notions of what things mean, how they are being expressed, or who else is there? Do they use the NKJV or the NIV and you prefer the XYZ? Kids, it's time for a humility check. It's all about LOVE. Love for God, love for worshiping Him, love for the others who are there (translate – respect) and obedience to be faithful and in communion with other Christians.

"I will worship toward Your holy temple,
And praise Your name
For Your lovingkindness and Your truth;
For You have magnified Your word
above all Your name."
~Psalm 138(139):2

Yes, we want to grow in our Faith. If we show up, He will work within us. Yes, we want to feel "fed." We want to feel blessed. It will come, if our heart is in the right place, and it will be from the Holy Spirit at the very core of our being. It won't be a warm fuzzy feeling based on a superficial emotion that makes you feel spiritual.

Gosh, we were having so much fun until this chapter. Then she ruined it. Get her a pulpit.

Have you ever gone to a counselor? It's an interesting process. You meet and make a decision to put your sanity in his or her hands. After the first meeting, you feel good. Or at least I did. The second meeting, "Why am I wasting my time?" The third meeting, "Why am I wasting my time and my money?" Then, if you're still faithful, the fourth meeting....LIFE CHANGING REVELATIONS AND CLARITY that leave you full of hope and a future! Fifth meeting, "Why am I doing this? Why isn't this like last time?" Then, several sessions later... SHAZAAM again!

Or how about reading the Bible? Your first time reading a verse when you are 10 years old, "OK, whatever that means, I'm reading my Bible like I was told." So many people stop here because they are frustrated about not understanding it, even into adulthood! But then, the second time reading the verse, "OK, yes I see how it relates to this Bible study material." Third time reading the verse, "SHAZAAM!" LIFE CHANGING! Down the road something happens, and the verse just pops into your head. That is the Holy Spirit revealing to you what you need to know when your heart is in the right place and you are ready for it.

One doesn't need to go far to see God's great faithfulness to us in Scripture. Being faithful to God is what going to church and worshiping is all about, along with being a faithful member of the body of Christ, as we are called to be.

"For as we have many members in one body, but all the members do not have the same function, so we, being many, are one body in Christ, and individual-

ly members of one another. Having then gifts differing according to the grace that is given to us, let us use them: if prophecy, let us prophesy in proportion to our faith; or ministry, let us use it in our ministering; he who teaches, in teaching; he who exhorts, in exhortation; he who gives, with liberality; he who leads, with diligence; he who shows mercy, with cheerfulness."
~Romans 12:4-5

Based on the Scripture above, Paul is saying that body parts cannot be separated from one another at will. If God has given me the gift of leadership, and I do not show up at church to lead, am I not squandering this gift, as did the servant given the talents in Matthew 25? And like the parable of the Ten Virgins, also in Matthew 25, we do not know when the Bridegroom will come for his Bride, the Church. However, let us say it happens during a set day and time of corporate worship. Will we be worshiping and waiting for Him with oil in our lamps? Or will we be in bed, at our lake house, or at a child's soccer game? If we are living as though He is not our God, even though we profess Him as such, Lord have mercy and forgive us our lack of faithfulness!

"And this is my prayer, that your love may abound more and more in knowledge and depth of insight, so that you may be able to discern what is best and be pure and blameless until the day of Christ."
~Phil 1:9-10

Are you emotionally uplifted or emotionally spent? I think we've all had those days/weeks when you feel like the energy has drained and you're walking around in circles. When was the last time you felt this way? It may have been last week or last year. There are many areas to look at when this happens. The big question is how to analyze the issues and dig ourselves out. Maybe it is temporary, and has to do with your body fighting off a cold. It could be a situation with your family that needed attending to. Or, maybe the culprit is the basic need to incorporate a lifestyle change.

Do you ever feel:

- Like you are not being faithful to yourself?
- That your life is out of control and you are drowning in it?
- What you used to think was fun, just isn't any longer?
- That your scheduled "fun" is just one more thing to cross off of your daily to do list?

If you are to that point now and want to design a life that is balanced, healthy, and full of joy, the key is in living out a life that is faithful to your beliefs and priorities....and leaving everything else behind.

What are your priorities? Make a list of what is important to you, and what you value in life. I have a feeling that this list will echo biblical principles of what God teaches us is important. This list becomes the framework of priorities that you should build your life around. List them in order of importance. Take number one. Are you living in accordance to your number one belief/priority? If not, this is where you start! What changes need to be made? What things need to be given up? I am embarrassed to tell you how many years I professed God to be my number one priority and didn't live a life that reflected this. Not only was this neglecting God, but it showed a lack of faithfulness to myself at the same time.

Since I'm more of a thinker type and less of a feeler (Myers-Briggs flashback), I like to take a business approach and do a SWOT analysis. Strengths and Weaknesses come from within; Opportunities and Threats are external influences. Let's start with number one on your list.

This would be a great time to use your journal!

Strengths

What are you doing now that supports this priority? Are you so committed to this priority that you are willing to do whatever it takes? Do you have a history of already making this priority number one so that it's already a habit?

Weaknesses

What is keeping you from living out this priority? Is it in you or are you being influenced externally? Maybe you have a false belief that something can't be changed? Is it a habit that you need to break? Are you too easily influenced by others? Are you so unhealthy physically that you lack the strength to live out your life the way you want to?

Opportunities

What is available to you? What could change? Is there someone to guide you or someone who could be a resource to help you, point out the direction and inspire you? When you look at your days, is there a slot of time, an hour, 30 minutes, 10 minutes, to be faithful to this priority? Who is behind you and will support a refocusing of your life with this as your top priority?

Threats

Is something or someone holding you back? What thought, weakness, or temptation may be getting in the way? Maybe it is a person who wants to keep you from realizing your priority, or inadvertently doesn't understand it, so they are a negative force in your life.

This may sound too simplified or too intense depending on your personality, but the key is to take action. Don't settle for a lifestyle that isn't faithful to who you are. It's yours to change! It takes work. It takes discernment. But most of all it takes loving yourself enough to act, and to know that you are no good to anyone if you don't practice faithfulness toward the lifestyle you are creating for yourself.

And when this happens to me? I have figured out the most important priorities are typically missing. I've been skipping my morning prayers. I've been eating poorly. I've been missing my exercise routine. I'm not scheduling my weeks according to my priorities. I'm letting life push me around! Faithfulness starts with being faithful to God, and manifests itself in a life that knows balance. A life in balance is a life of peace. Peace leads us to joy. To live your life according to your beliefs is to live it with control over yourself. And what's interesting is that control, which you develop, gives you freedom! Like a child who has a schedule and boundaries, it ends up giving us a sense of freedom and security.

> *"Whoever has no rule over his own spirit*
> *is like a city broken down, without walls."*
> ~*Proverbs 25:28*

A PHYSICAL VIEW OF FAITHFULNESS

I think of faithfulness as something that you do consistently that gives big results. The actions become habits, and the habits support your health. One of the things that I am faithful to is my body's need for water...which brings to mind a song...

> *"Raindrops on roses and whiskers on kittens,*
> *Bright copper kettles and warm woolen mittens,*
> *Brown paper packages tied up with strings...*
> *These are a few of my favorite things!"*

The study of Macrobiotics teaches us to start each day with a happy song. This has become one of my favorite things. Another one of my favorite things is water. I was sold on the importance of drinking a lot of water at age 17, and it was the reason I lost my BFF at the time. See, I just couldn't watch her drink a diet soda every morning for breakfast, so I felt like I had to let her know how bad it was, and that she should be drinking water. I couldn't help myself! Honestly, I cared about her, and just wanted to help, even though I'm sure I was irritating. Looking back, I can see that becoming a Health Coach was my destiny. Learning about the benefits of water and stopping all soda consumption at 17 was the start of my love for health and wellness.

Whenever I tell people to drink half their weight in ounces of water a day, I typically get three responses which I'll list here along with my tips:

I don't like the taste of it: Well, first of all, it must be clean water. By clean I mean no fluoride, no chlorine - all of the bad stuff that is bad tasting filtered out. What's left is pure God given goodness. Squeeze a lemon into it and you have the added advantage of reducing the acid in your body which is a breeding ground for bacteria and encourages disease. Put a little pure unsweetened cranberry juice in it and get those toxins in the fast lane of the highway to elimination. By balancing the acidity in your body along with drinking pure water you are taking a huge step to wellness right there! Add in a drop of essential oil. Maybe wild orange for pep, or even a little Melaleuca if you are feeling like you might be coming down with something. If you are adding essential oils, make sure your bottle is glass or stainless steel. Oils have been known to eat into plastic.

I'll spend all of my time in the bathroom: Yes, you will – at first. See, if you aren't getting enough water, your body thinks that it is in survival mode. It's stashing away any drop it can get from food or the occasional glass consumed when taking a pill. But the bathroom breaks will taper off after a while as your body realizes that it isn't going to die. Really! And most people even lose weight! I really think that people must stop thinking that normal body functions are an inconvenience. I just want to say, slow down, sit down, think about all of those toxins that are being flushed out, and sing a happy song! Not that I quote Martha Stewart very often, but, using the restroom… "It's a good thing!"

I don't have time or energy to keep track of how much water I drink: Me neither. I believe water should be an accessory. That's why I carry around a 64oz jug everywhere I go. It's like my bright green blankie. My green water jug sits on my desk and I sip from it all day. I take it in the car, onto the tennis court, and SHAZAAM! I reach for it without even thinking and there is nothing left. Just like that. When that happens to you, you'll know you've arrived! Today I went to a nice restaurant with my friends and it was sitting there on the table in front of me. Sort of tacky, but whatever, there's no telling what is in restaurant water, so better safe than sorry. If you are flushing out toxins, it doesn't make sense to consume them at the same time.

WATER = LIFE

After three days your body starts shutting down without it. It keeps organs functioning correctly, wards off sickness and disease, nourishes skin and keeps blood flowing efficiently. In the past 35 years, since being sold on water the first time, no study has come out to replace or refute the scientific knowledge we have about the key role water plays in our health.

But, you say, if I'm drinking all of this water, when will I have time for a soda? EXACTLY!

While I'm preaching, I now feel compelled to talk about sports drinks. Goodbye Gatorade and all of your unhealthy counterparts!

How many of you have been told by people you trust that you should drink a sports drink to replace your electrolytes? How many people think that sports drinks are a healthy and legitimate beverage; if you are a sports-minded person, or sick with the flu?

Have you looked at the ingredient list? You have more to fear from the junk in these drinks than you do from many of the reasons you drink them. Of course, if you feel faint and all you have at your fingertips is red, yellow or blue dyed chemical concoctions, I guess I understand. But that's where planning ahead comes in handy.

My beverage of choice is coconut water, which I like to call "God's original sports drink." It has more potassium than a banana, naturally occurring electrolytes, sodium, and naturally occurring sugars. Plan ahead for sports events, sickness, or even mowing your lawn in 90 degree weather and put some in your refrigerator!

But caution! As with every single thing that you buy at the grocery store, don't put it in your cart without reading the ingredient list! While searching the "health food" aisles, I found many that had yuck in them. However, I did find Vita Coco. The pure coconut version is an acquired taste but the flavored versions with added fruit (yes, just fruit) taste great and even kids will think they are wonderful. I caution you from drinking too much of it, like 32 ounces, as it may have a laxative effect. And of course, as with most things, you can make your own sports drinks from basic ingredients and save a lot of money.

CHALLENGES AND JOURNALING OPPORTUNITIES

I know, I know. First I put you on an eating plan, then I make you commit to exercise, and now with the water. I'll be lucky if this book doesn't end up on the shelf right now or on Amazon for $1.37!

- Make sure you're drinking the right amount of water this week and going forward. What was the biggest thing you noticed? What is your favorite thing to put in it, if anything? Try putting in some lemon or lime to help alkalize your system, and ward off inflammation and disease at the same time.

- Do a SWOT analysis in your journal and share your top priorities.

- Share with others, when has Shazaam happened to you?

- I've mentioned that water equals life in a physical sense. I'd like you to ponder and journal about this conversation between a man in India known for his wisdom and Mother Gavrilia:

"Who is your God?"

MG: "There is only one God, and Christ is his son. This is my God!"

"I guessed as much. But why don't you say it? It is the first time that we see a European who doesn't talk, who doesn't tell us that our gods are nothing. You see our life, you know our philosophy, but you make no comments. How is that? Missionaries are always reproving then go away; criticize then leave."

MG: "I cannot say such things, because our ancestors were like you!"

"What do you mean by that?"

MG: "So I started to talk about the ancient Greeks and explained how, when Christianity reached our country, it did not make us renounce all of our ancient philosophy, but gave us Christ as life. Because Christ is not only a religion. Christ is life."

Gentleness

—— ∽ ——

Hebrew
הָוְנַע or Anvah

Greek
πραΰτης or Prautés

—— ∽ ——

*(Now the man Moses was very humble, more than all men
who were on the face of the earth.)*

Numbers 12:3

Gentleness

———— ∾ ————

I n English translations, gentle, meek, and humble are often interchangeable. The words are best defined as when someone who has the power, authority or knowledge to put you in your place, chooses not to. Humility is also a good word.

We know that God made Moses one of the most powerful men on earth, and that He had direct communication with him. Gentleness is embodied by only the strongest people. Quite contrary to what our culture tells us!

> *"I, therefore, the prisoner of the Lord, beseech you to walk worthy of the calling with which you were called, with all lowliness and gentleness, with long-suffering, bearing with one another in love, endeavoring to keep the unity of the Spirit in the bond of peace."*
>
> *~Ephesians 4:1-3*

The spiritual and emotional side of gentleness is so finely intertwined for me. I cannot help but see God's gentleness, especially as He brought it to us in His Son, and not immediately jump to knowing that our spiritual and emotional health rely on our ability to understand gentleness. It manifests itself in how we can control our emotions, what we say and how we act. Gentleness is the opposite of pride. Humility leads to gentleness.

Jesus epitomized it. How could He not? He was God Himself Incarnate. When you see how he interacted with others, you see a man who acted only out of love.

A man whose only mission was to save His people, and this mission dictated everything he said and did. There was no sign of pride or lack of humility. And yet, it is so hard for us!

> *"Rejoice in the Lord always. Again I will say, rejoice!*
> *"Let your gentleness be known to all men. The Lord is at hand.*
> *"Be anxious for nothing, but in everything by prayer and supplication, with thanksgiving, let your requests be made known to God; and the peace of God, which surpasses all understanding, will guard your hearts and minds through Christ Jesus."*
> *~Philippians 4:4-7*

I'll never forget a dinner I had with some co-workers back in 2007. We were sitting in a restaurant, and somehow the conversation turned to God. There were four of us at the table and each of us professed our belief. I was at a table with an Orthodox Jew, a practicing Wicca, a gentleman who believed in the Universe, but said he didn't believe in God, and a "Recovering Catholic." Now, I had been quite spoiled, since in my previous company I was surrounded by practicing Christians. I was a little in shock, but what made the most impact on me was the "Recovering Catholic." He said that Christianity was full of hypocrites and for the weak. He saw his grandmother repeatedly turn to God when things got tough instead of facing things full on. (Pause for effect) I'll let this sink in.

What? Yes, it's so easy to have faith in someone you can't see and touch physically. It's so easy to leave your burdens in Another's Hands and wait. It's so easy to see terrible things happen all around you and know that God is in control. It's so easy to see your sins hurt people and yourself, confess these sins and vow never to let them happen again, only to see them happen again. It's so easy to push aside the guilt and know that you are forgiven by Someone who you can't physically see and touch. I think you get it, and I know I'm singing to the choir. This sarcastic ranting doesn't sound very gentle, I know. Thinking of him with love and praying for him would have been the correct and gentle response. I imagine his grandmother as I do many other grandmothers who make it look so easy. Now, THEY embody gentleness! Sometimes, like Moses, it takes a lifetime to make it look easy.

Many translations of Galatians 5:23 use the word meekness instead of gentleness, and the memory above makes me think of Paul using both words when he wrote to the Corinthians.

> *Now I, Paul, myself am pleading with you by the meekness and gentleness of Christ—who in presence am lowly among you, but being absent am bold toward you...*
>
> *~2 Corinthians 10:1*

This reminds me of myself. When I was sitting at the dinner table, across from the man who was basically telling me that I was a weak hypocrite, I just looked at him with understanding (hopefully that was the look on my face) and told him that I was sorry that he had that impression of Christians. But you see how I respond now with boldness in a book he'll never read! Cynthia, at your age, you are still struggling. Moses, again, the meekest man on earth, gives me hope.

The meek shall inherit the earth. Meek may rhyme with weak, and look the same to some people, but they are polar opposites! Meekness and gentleness have to do with humility, and I for one struggle with this. My friends, we must all do exactly the opposite of what the world tells us to do in cases like these. We're told to stand up for ourselves. Don't let people walk all over you! Set people straight! Don't let someone get away with that!

Push, push, push! Instead, the Bible implores us not to worry. Take a couple deep breaths and know that God will take care of it. Trust that He will show others the way, gently, and in the way that they need to hear it. He will give us rest in our souls. Who doesn't want that? Just writing it makes me long for it. He doesn't call us to be in conflict with others, He calls us to pray for them.

I do agree that He puts certain people in positions to stand up for the Faith, evangelize, exhort, and encourage our fellow man to see the Light. But I've found that far too many people take on this responsibility, and out of zeal alienate others when prayer and gentleness would have sufficed. Do you feel led to stand on a street corner and get into "theological" talks or arguments with people? Do you feel put on the spot at times, and later feel that you should have "stood up for Christ," as they say? How gentle, meek, and humble are we in a world that encourages, and even values pride and assertiveness?

During an interview with Mother Gavrilia:
"We must not judge others. Still, we must know that if we do not judge others, all the others will judge us for that. Once I happened to give a talk on various events and, when I had finished, the comment was: "But she did not condemn these, she did not condemn those, she did not condemn the others, etc." Well? Have you understood? You will be judged for not judging others."

Question: What are we to do then?

Mother Gavrilia: Exactly that: You must not care if you are judged.

Question: And when we hear people judging others?

Mother Gavrilia: Take no part in the conversation.

Brethren, if a man is overtaken in any trespass, you who are spiritual restore such a one in a spirit of gentleness, considering yourself lest you also be tempted. Bear one another's burdens, and so fulfill the law of Christ. For if anyone thinks himself to be something, when he is nothing, he deceives himself.

~Galatians 6:1-3

A PHYSICAL VIEW OF GENTLENESS

Study upon study has proven that multitasking has gotten way out of control. Similar to windows opening up on browsers, and open tabs lining the top of our screens, our brains are working as fast as they can to keep up with everything we want to do. Right. This. Minute. Women have been applauded over the years for their ability to multitask better than men. It's true, our brains are wired this way. Thus, the commentary goes, it makes us better at running households and taking care of children. I'm not saying that it isn't useful. Seeing Sarah toddle toward the stairs while preventing Billy from experimenting with the dials on the stove, while making dinner and taking a phone call is all in a day's work for some women. Other women who are single, without children and/or work outside of the home, are basically doing the same things, but the age of the people and the tasks are different.

"My soul, wait silently for God alone, for my expectation is from Him."
~Psalm 62(63):5

The problem is, we don't know when to stop and turn it off. Which leads to the issue of multi-tasking actually turning into obsessive compulsive behavior. You don't want to do two things at once, but you can't help yourself. When this starts affecting your loved ones, anxiety sets in, tempers flare, and there is anything but gentleness in our lives. Sure, I can listen to you and check Facebook at the same time. Talk on the phone while checking emails? Yes, I am Superwoman and can give 100% of my brain to each. Or is it, no, I'm not Superwoman, but you don't deserve 100% of my attention. Ouch.

Studies have been showing for years, that you are actually less efficient due to making mistakes and having to redo your work. You miss important details. Emotions and cues from others are missed, so relationships break down. Also, clarity of mind becomes so muddled so that thoughts and ideas cannot be articulated. We are in the middle of both a communication and an efficiency crisis. There is anything but gentleness going on in a typical day. We need to slow down and think again. We need to slow down and listen. If we do not have peace and order within ourselves, we cannot extend the same to others. It starts internally, within us.

"The hour through which you are at present passing, the man whom you meet here and now, the task on which you are engaged at this very moment — these are always the most important in your whole life."
~P. Evdokimov

I have two prescriptions that can help. The first is to go off on a spiritual retreat now and again. It may only be for a few hours, one day when the kids are at school. It may be a day off of work, solely for the purpose of committing to self-inspection. It could be a quiet weekend at a monastery. Whatever you can do, your soul will thank you with a sense of peace that precedes gentleness.

"Man does not retreat from the world to find God. He does it to discover himself. And when he discovers himself, then he can stand before God, repentant, humble, a nobody, who begins little by little to recognize and reject the many evils he had collected through his pride; through his social contacts; through

his vanity, encouraged by compliments and praises. Then he can truly understand who he really is. We know from the Ancients, that what is most important is to know thyself. To the very end of our life, only a scrutiny of ourselves may reveal the extent of our union with God."

~Mother Gavrilia

———————————— ✍ ————————————

The other is a daily practice called mindful meditation, or practicing mindfulness. It's quite trendy today, but it is actually something that's been around for centuries, and has been practiced by people from all walks of life regardless of religion. Mindfulness can re-introduce gentleness, and its cousin, peace, into your life. Combined with breathing exercises, there are many physical and psychological benefits.

Neuroscientists observing MRI scans have learned that meditation strengthens the brain by reinforcing the connections between brain cells. Dr. Herbert Benson is a cardiologist who has been studying the health effects of meditation over three decades for Harvard Medical School. He says that any condition that's caused or worsened by stress can be alleviated through meditation. The relaxation response helps decrease metabolism, lowers blood pressure, and improves heart rate, breathing, and brain waves," Benson says. Tension and tightness seep from muscles as the body receives a quiet message to relax. Mindfulness meditation has also been found to increase levels of empathy, and helps train wandering minds to focus, which is helpful with ADD patients.

It's easy to get lost in non-Christian beliefs while studying mindfulness, meditation and breathing. I would like to keep the focus on Christ, as our Christian monastics do, who practice hesychia, which means "the prayer of the heart." We will not be emptying our heads or trying to reach an "enlightened state," but instead our minds will be quiet enough to allow us to hear the Holy Spirit.

"Finally, brethren, whatever things are true, whatever things are noble, whatever things are just, whatever things are pure, whatever things are lovely, whatever things are of good report, if there is any virtue and if there is anything praiseworthy—meditate on these things."

~Philippians 4:8

Whenever the Bible refers to meditation, it refers to, not an empty mind, but a focus on God and His Word. We are realizing the God given synergistic benefits of becoming more energized, releasing stress, improving our ability to focus and communicate, and be creative. We are even improving organ function. I love how Father John Breck puts it so well in this quote…

"Silence and stillness are essential to attain spiritual knowledge, to engage in spiritual warfare against the passions and against demonic powers, and to allow the voice of God to be heard. Silence and stillness nevertheless require a certain solitude, a temporary withdrawing from the noise and busyness of the world that cause endless distractions and hinder us in our quest for God."

Mindfulness involves observing things that are happening around you without evaluating, judging, or participating. Mindful meditation is focusing on the present moment. I know that this can be extremely difficult! It's hard work. You will be tempted to stop doing what feels like nothing, and start wondering what you are having for dinner. Persevere. You are worth this small ten minute break. When this happens to me, I usually pray, Lord Have Mercy, The Jesus Prayer, or bring Scripture to mind, then I go back to listening to my breath. When it happens again, oh, I need to remember to call so-and-so…I pray for the person who comes to mind, and then go back to my breath. That's where it begins, with just listening to your breath and feeling how it's cooler coming in through the nose and warmer going out through the mouth. This is called "breath work."

Start in a sitting position with your back straight and your feet flat on the floor. Relax your arms. I like to use Dr. Andrew Weil's method of inhaling through the nose for 4 counts, holding for 7 counts and exhaling for 8 counts through your mouth making a whoosh sound, keeping your tongue touching the tissue right behind your front teeth. You are exhaling more carbon dioxide that you take in as oxygen. He isn't sure why the tongue position is important, but this was passed down through the Hindu practice, so he does it. He recommends doing this 2 times a day and starting with only 4 breaths. Dr. Weil also says that it is the regularity of doing it 2 times a day that produces the benefits, not the one time a week, when you have time to squeeze it in approach.

Science has shown us that the exchange of oxygen with carbon dioxide is naturally calming.

One more step that I would like you to think about as you progress in a breathing practice involves your diaphragm and your lymphatic system. Our lymphatic system is one vehicle our body uses to release waste and toxins from our cells. By keeping it moving, we are able to flush out harmful waste that can build up and make us sick. One way to do this is through deep diaphragmatic breathing. When you take a deep breath in, slowly push your belly out. As your diaphragm moves, your internal organs are massaged and your lymphatic system does what it's meant to do. It's often helpful to put one hand on your stomach and one on your heart to monitor which part of your body is moving with each breath.

CHALLENGES AND JOURNALING OPPORTUNITIES

- Can you recall a time when you could have been gentler? What were the ramifications? Is there an ongoing situation that pushes your gentleness button to the off position? How can you hit "reset?"

- Set aside one time a day to start a breathing practice. Do you think this is not for you? Please try it for a week and see what happens. I like to combine mine with praying the hours, which is a monastic tradition of remembering God as we go about our day. Set your alarm button on your phone if you need to. Take at least 5 minutes to let the practice calm you and bring you back to what is important, namely God in His right place in your day, and what is expected of you in the moment. Get back to us with what you experienced!

- If you would like to pray the hours, here is a brief outline of what that would entail. I've found praying the hours to be a particular blessing on those infrequent days when I can stay home and retreat from the world. Something I would like you to keep in mind, is that while these are personal prayers, and we can relate them to our current day, they are also prayers and remembrance for the whole Christian body of believers, the Church.

FIRST HOUR

"To You I pray, O Lord; in the morning You hear my voice!"

~Psalm 5

The hours used to start at sunrise. Now, they typically start at 6 a.m. During the first hour, we pray that God bless our day and that He will guard us from everything that could harm us, both body and soul. We ask Him to enlighten our souls with His love and wisdom for the coming day.

Read Psalm 5

THIRD HOUR

"Do not take Your Holy Spirit from me."

~Psalm 51

The third hour is around 9 a.m. At this time, we remember the Apostles, and how the Holy Spirit, the Comforter came down upon them, and we thank Him for this Gift. We open our hearts to His continued guidance and sanctification, and pray that we keep the knowledge of His presence beside us throughout our day.

Read Psalm 25

SIXTH HOUR

"There they crucified Him...It was now about the sixth hour."

~*Luke 23:33, 44*

The sixth hour falls at noon. If you pray at this time, you will be joining many churches throughout the world in a special remembrance of God's great sacrifice for us in the crucifixion of His Son. We are sorrowful, but we rejoice, for by His great love, we have salvation.

Read Psalm 54

NINTH HOUR

"And at the ninth hour...Jesus cried out with a loud voice, and breathed His last."

~*Mark 15:34, 37*

We close the prayer of the hours at 3 p.m., when Christ breathed His last breath. We pray with thankfulness that He is still with us, although His physical body is not. He was with us all day, and will be all night. He never leaves our side.

Read Psalm 84

Self-control

---∽---

Hebrew
תּוֹעֵינְצ (Tzeniut) (Modesty)

Greek
ἐγκράτεια (enkrateia) (Inner Strength)

---∽---

*But also for this very reason, giving all diligence, add
to your faith virtue, to virtue knowledge, to knowledge
self-control, to self-control perseverance, to perseverance
godliness, to godliness brotherly kindness; and to brotherly
kindness love.*

2 Peter 1:5-7

Self-control

―――――∽―――――

Rita Madden gives us a great perspective on the subject of self-control and its many facets.

Self-control: it's something we're sure we don't have enough of; we're convinced the person next to us has more of; and we wish we could buy it in a bottle.

How many times do we find ourselves wishing that a struggle of ours would just go away?

Okay, I snacked way too much today. Please help me resist the snacking habit.

Okay, I snapped at way too many co-workers today. Please help me cool down my anger.

Okay, I've been lazy for a week straight. Please help me get moving.

We're good at asking, but we seem to get tripped up when it comes to acting.

My husband is an expert at keeping the house organized. He's always telling me, "If you put something back right after using it, you won't need to set aside a block of time to organize the house." It's painful for me to admit that he's right.

Where is my self-control in the area of tidiness? Putting something away after I'm done with it is not part of my way of doing things. I'm not as neat and tidy as he is, and it's downright frustrating. I look at him and think: Why does he have more self-control in the tidiness area than I have?

I see him working at it. He often explains to me that he feels less stressed when the house is in order. Therefore, when he's done using something, he puts it away immediately. He uses his tendency to keep things tidy as a way to manage his stress.

Even though my husband is able to keep the house organized, I could mention a long list of items on which he needs to practice more self-control. But formulating such a list and making it public would likely start an unnecessary marital dispute, and I can do without that.

Often I think about the people who are dedicated to exercise and especially running. Their alarms go off in the morning; then they're outside jogging: rain or shine.

How do they do it? (Personally, I'm not a runner. In fact, the only time you'll catch me running is if someone is chasing me.) But I wonder: do these dedicated runners have days when the alarm goes off and they just want to stay in bed?

Certainly, many runners tend to be well-disciplined persons, but it's quite possible that some runners who are committed to their morning jogs might be struggling in other areas. An example could well be: anger in the workplace, an emotion that needs to be under control.

The point of all this is: We all have our personal struggles and issues that need to be under control. We might be aware of them and admit them, or we might overlook them, but they are there. None of us is free from them.

The *Merriam-Webster Dictionary* defines self-control as: "restraint exercised over one's own impulses, emotions, or desires."

The key word here is "exercised." Self-control is not something that just falls from the sky (boy, do I wish that were the case, though); rather, it is something that through grace we work with God to exercise.

On what do we need to exercise self-control? Should I start with my personal list now? Better not, for this book would be longer than Tolstoy's *War and Peace*.

Seriously, we see the need for self-control when we're trying *not* to give in to the many temptations that come our way, among them: overeating; anger; idle talk; excessive Internet posting, reading, and surfing; overuse of technology; compulsive shopping; laziness; lack of praying; and the list, as we well know, can go on and on.

Now, we know that temptation is not a sin, for Christ was tempted, and He is the only one without sin. We also know that temptation is part of the fallen world, and in this earthly life, temptation will always be with us until the end. Elder Ieronymos of Aegina reminds us:

> *"The evil one cannot comprehend the joy we receive from the spiritual life; for this reason he is jealous of us, he envies us and sets traps for us, and we become grieved and fall. We must struggle, because without struggles we do not obtain virtues."*

As much as we wish it, we know that God is not going to make our struggles, our bad habits, our evil impulses, our wicked emotions, or unhealthy desires go away by throwing on them some pixie dust. God is not going to take away our ability to make choices. We need to work with God to overcome and *not* to give in to our temptations.

When we pray The Lord's Prayer, what do we ask God? We ask him to lead us *not* into temptation. And He whispers to us, "fair request, but work with me." We need to pause and take time to examine ourselves. St. Thalassios the Libyan advises us:

> *"If you wish to be in control of your soul and body, forestall the passions by rooting out their causes."*

Let me put all this in a good news-bad news formula: the bad news is, we're going to be tempted and fall. The good news is, when we fall we can get back up. The best news is: God will forgive us, will never leave us, and if we want Him to, He will faithfully work with us! God is with us!

122

The first step in exercising self-control is to examine ourselves. It is a call to repentance. Through true repentance, we recognize what we do not want to do. We see our brokenness and sin, and we recognize our dependence on God. To truly repent, we need the desire to rid ourselves of the detrimental action and to align ourselves with God's will, to examine ourselves, and come to understand why we are falling into the behavior, and then to formulate a plan to turn away from the action.

The ancient Christian church emphasizes that moving away from a bad habit is not going to happen without struggle or effort. They emphasize that we'll be contending with our passions in the flesh, and we'll be struggling against the evil one and his darts and demons.

That bottle of self-control that we wish we could purchase (even if we had to pay full price,) doesn't exist. It's time to accept the fact, as hard as that is to do, that such a bottle is not for sale, and we need to work diligently to attain the fruits of our labor. Yes, self-control is going to require us to exercise effort on our part. We need and must show restraint when we are tempted.

However, we are not in this alone. Our heavenly Father desires and wants to work with us, aiding us in acquiring this fruit of the spirit: self-control. In this context, we could well envision the icon (a term for "picture" or "image" in the Orthodox Christian Tradition) of the Resurrection in a fresh way: in it, we can see Christ stretching out His hand, pulling us out of the tombs of our sin, raising us up to partake in Him.

Now, let's explore some tangible things in which we can make self-control a tool that we exercise more and more in order to become holistic women—with the ultimate goal being to work toward attaining union and likeness with God.

A PHYSICAL VIEW OF
SELF-CONTROL

Since we are all working on different areas of self-control, I thought it would be helpful to highlight some common areas that many of us can benefit from. But generally speaking, controlling oneself requires focus and reflection on the unwanted action, impulse, emotion, or desire. It requires a thoughtful and realistic way to change those unwanted states. We might ask ourselves: Are there specific barriers in our way that will prevent us from changing those states? If so, what can we do to remove those barriers? In other words: How can we exercise self-control?

Whatever we do to achieve self-control, we need to remember to set realistic goals. Sometimes when the mark is set too high, it makes it very difficult for us to attain what we are trying to achieve. Let's look at two areas (eating and stress) that we could consider working on during the days ahead.

Eating
Snacking
Snacking throughout the day is one of the easiest ways to consume unnecessary calories. There are proper times for snacks, and snacks should be made up of foods that are nutrient dense. A snack is not a cookie or ice cream. These are "treat foods," and they need to be placed in their proper context. There is nothing wrong with enjoying a "treat food," but again having it in its proper time is key, and doing that in itself an act of self-control.

It is wise to focus on trying to cut out—or at least cut down—between-meal snacking. Yes, there are times a snack is appropriate, and it could be taken then. But contrary to popular belief, feeling the discomfort of hunger (that might lead to a snack) is actually an acceptable state in a person's daily life.

When we feel physically hungry and allow ourselves to experience hunger pains, we are in effect participating in a form of fasting, and fasting is a tool to aid us in emptying ourselves of our physical desires, making us aware of our dependence on God. It is a tool to deepen us in our prayer life. When we are hungry, this is a physical cue to aid us in turning to God in prayer. Saying no to an unnecessary snack is an exercise in self-control. The wisdom of the Desert Fathers speaks to this point:

> *"A brother felt hungry at dawn, and struggled not to eat till nine o'clock. When nine o'clock came, he made himself wait till noon. At noon he dipped his bread and sat down to eat, but then got up again, saying, "I will wait till three." At eight o'clock he prayed and saw the devil's work going out of him like smoke; and his hunger ceased."*

Moving away from snacking benefits us both in a physical and a spiritual way. Simply put, we should exercise restraint (self-control) from snacking and move away from it. But if we're new to this approach of *not* snacking between meals, then some guidelines are helpful. A good starter gauge might be to try going at least 5 hours between meals without snacking. At the end of the fifth hour, if our next meal is going to be approximately two hours away or even longer, and then if we're truly feeling hungry, this would be an appropriate time for a snack. But if our next meal is going to be within an hour or so, it would be worth trying—indeed, it would be wise—to go without a snack. This process of restraint exercised over our snacking impulses requires us to do some self-reflection on why we feel we want a snack: much research suggests we're snacking for reasons other than true hunger.

Now what should we do to trim the temptation to snack? Will we need to remove "snack" foods from our home or workstation? Do we tend to snack in the evening? If so, coming up with a different evening plan in which our hands are occupied could be a strategy to aid us in decreasing snacking. Or, we may try pushing back dinner and eating a little later in order to avoid late-night snacking. In all of this, we need to exercise, consciously exercise, restraint or self-control over our habit or impulse to snack.

Related to snacking is the matter of portion control in eating.

Portion Control

We all know that dreaded over-the-edge bite. It's the bite that officially ruins the meal. We leave the table feeling uncomfortably stuffed, tired, and irritated with a bellyache. St. John Chrysostom reminds us:

"Eat just enough to alleviate your hunger."

In a recent study conducted at Cornell University and published in the *International Journal of Obesity*, researchers demonstrated that adults eat an average of 92% of what they put on their plates. That means if we put more on our plates than our body needs, we are likely to eat it and take those couple extra bites that our body does not need, just because it is in front of us.

Dr. Brian Wansink, a researcher of the study, notes that this finding is very helpful because "Just knowing that you're likely to consume almost all of what you serve yourself can help you be more mindful of appropriate portion size."

A good exercise in self-control would be to put less food on our plate than we think we want. If we really need to, we can always go back for more. But what we need to remember here is this: If the food is in front of us, we will eat it, so we need to practice self-control at meal time by serving ourselves a little bit less. We don't need to drastically cut our portions by serving ourselves half of what we usually eat. But we must serve ourselves a bit less.

Let's look at an example: if we usually eat 2 cups of food, we don't want to go from 2 cups to 1 cup, but maybe we should think about going from 2 cups to 1 ¾ cup. We need to take just a tiny bit less than we usually serve ourselves or we think we want. We need to always remember that we can go back for more, but the reality of it is: if it's in front of us, we'll eat it.

Besides snacking and portion control in eating, stress management is an area in our lives that could use some self-control.

STRESS MANAGEMENT

Current research indicates that when we are not managing the stress in our lives, the region of our brain that is involved with emotions and self-control becomes damaged. Managing the stress in our life is another area that can benefit us when it comes to self-control.

Whether we tend to get angry quickly with others, sleep too much (or too little), struggle with motivation, or have portion-control problems when it comes to eating, managing stress can be a tool to help us in these, and other areas.

We might also consider making an appointment with ourselves to do something that will help us manage stress. We could make time to read an enjoyable book, go for a meditative walk, enjoy a cup of tea with a friend, watercolor, sing, dance, garden, or listen to our favorite music. These and other activities will help us manage stress.

Also, and perhaps more importantly, we will be well-advised to practice committing to a prayer rule in our prayer corner. *[Note: A prayer corner is the Christian tradition of a place in the home devoted to prayer. It could be a corner or a room. A prayer rule is a set of prayers that are said every day in that particular area of the home.]* Practicing silence is a form of prayer, and has been practiced by many as we see it passed down through Holy Tradition.

We could take five minutes a day just to sit in silence. We're are always so busy telling God what we want, but many times we need to silence ourselves to hear the voice of God. "Be still and know that I am God," the psalmist commands us in Psalm 46 verse 10.

Time in our prayer corner is an act of self-control, for in being there, we give up time doing something else simply to be with God. Yes, we can pray and should pray at all times, but creating this time to pause during the day and honor our prayer rule will benefit us and others more than we are capable of understanding.

What will we have to do to get to our prayer corners? Will we need to get up a little bit earlier before heading to work? Will we have to forgo a morning check of Facebook after dropping the kids off at school? What are our barriers and what plan needs to be put into place to overcome them? These are the kind of questions that we need to ask ourselves as we search and seek ways to exercise restraint—self-control—on our emotions, desires, or stressful situations.

SELF-CONTROL STRATEGIES

Now, in general, when it comes to self-control there are a few tips to take note of:

Self-talk is helpful. That's right: we need sometimes to talk to ourselves; after all, there is only one person listening, and that person forms a pretty good audience of one. Here are examples of self-talk:

If we find ourselves standing at the refrigerator door wanting a snack and we're not really hungry, we should simply ask ourselves out loud: "What am I doing? Am I truly hungry? Can I wait it out till the next meal?" By asking ourselves these (and similar) questions, we may start to gain some understanding that we often want to eat out of boredom, emotions, habit, or frustration. It is a tool to initiate self-reflection on what many refer to as mindfulness in eating—a strategy to help us avoid mindless eating.

If we are frustrated with a co-worker or a family member and we just want to lash out at them, we might consider having a conversation with ourselves and try to examine the matter from all sides before we approach them. We should ask ourselves: "What am I really upset with? How can I communicate this in a way that is, in the words of Saint Paul, 'speaking the truth in love'?" Through this self-talk session, we may re-think and redefine our purpose for wanting to talk to them, and we will converse with them in a more thoughtful manner.

Prayer is necessary. Now after we have had our self-talk moments and we realize we need help, we can and should ASK for it! We can call on Christ to help us fight the temptation before us. You probably have earthly friends who would be willing to pray for you as you struggle to change your life and grow. We also have many heavenly helpers, in the Saints and angels, who are with us all the time, eager to help us attain union with Christ, yet we do not ask. We tend to neglect the tool of prayer especially when we need it most. Our helpers want to help. They want to work with us, so we need to seek out working with them.

Practice self-forgiveness. Many times we get so frustrated with ourselves when we fall that we keep ourselves pinned down as a result of unhealthy guilt. A spiritual mother once asked: "Why do people have such a hard time forgiving themselves? If God can forgive us, then why can't we forgive ourselves? Are we somehow better than God?"

John Climacus cautions us:

"Do not be surprised that you fall every day; do not give up, but stand your ground courageously. And assuredly, the angel who guards you will honor your patience."

If we fall while trying to practice self-control by restraining our impulses, emotions, or desires, we need to repent, forgive ourselves, and work on plans to help us change the unwanted way or ways. We know "falls" will come, but we have to remember that we can always get back up, and our loving Lord is always going to be there stretching out His arm to lift us back up.

CHALLENGES AND JOURNALING OPPORTUNITIES

- Let's take a moment to reflect and journal on an area in which we need to exercise more self-control. Implement the process of true repentance, and formulate a plan to turn away from the action. Consider the barriers that are in our way, and make sure we have strategies in place to overcome them. The examples above provide some suggestions. Topics from other chapters may come to mind. In fact, I hope they do!

- Did Rita Madden's way of describing stress, eating, and self-control create any "Aha!" moments?

Conclusion

W hen I first started writing this book, I thought it would be great to base it on the Fruit of the Spirit. At first it was easy. Ready-made chapters! Subjects that were definitive and focused. What could be better? Then it got confusing.

What I found was something that I had already studied in the past, but hadn't truly internalized. The Fruit of the Spirit is really one fruit, not nine. They intertwine with each other and form a thread that pulls together your mind, body, soul, and entire life and lifestyle. Each story I have shared with you has elements of each. At times it was difficult to know where to plug things in after the inspiration to write them. I would strategize - this is about love…no, peace…no, self-control…

There are many other components that weave into a thread that encompasses everything we do, stress, for instance. As every author shared, stress affects our health, relationships, mental capacity for learning, memory, and our spiritual life. By managing this one factor through eating, and lifestyle, we can find health, joy, and purpose in our lives. We've all heard about how God opens doors for us, or closes, them depending on His plan. But sometimes we have to build the doors. Don't worry, He can still lock them, but He has definitely given us the tools.

You CAN take control of your life. You are empowered by God to make choices that affect you positively or negatively. The key is to know what is in your control, do what is in your control, and leave the rest to Him. He has given us the tools to use in all areas, and He outlines and points us to them in Scripture. While you are here on this earth, are you living the way God intended? If you are running around overwhelmed, grabbing meals from drive-thrus on the way to obligations that leave you spent without quality time for yourself or family, maybe not. If you aren't sleeping, are overweight, feel rundown, and have out of control cravings, maybe not. If it feels like your life is running you instead of the other way around, maybe not. If you are so busy that your priorities are mixed up and you are missing prayer time, devotions, and worship, maybe not. Maybe I should take out the "maybes"?

I urge those of you who are struggling with change to look into hiring a health coach. Yes, it is an expense, but the expense of future healthcare costs, the stress of hospitalizations, and a life lived with regret and pain makes the investment a small drop in the bucket. Studies have shown that 98% of people cannot reach their goals without outside help. It may come from a friend or family member, doctor or other professional, but it surely isn't something to feel guilty about if you can't achieve it by yourself. As we have covered, we are created to be in relationship with each other. That is my hope and prayer. That the relationship we have had through this book was helpful and thought provoking, that your life is better for reading it, and that you were able to learn something from my knowledge as a holistic health professional and my personal experiences.

Here are some tips for hiring Certified Holistic Health Coaches:

Make sure that they are certified through a reputable school. They may have the title "Certified Integrative Nutrition Health Coach.: Currently, there are federal guidelines being created for this relatively new profession, as there are some who go by a self-described "Health Coach" title without training.

Work with someone who feels right to you. Most health coaches offer complimentary health consultations. This is not just an exercise for them to go over your health history and the packages they offer. It's an opportunity for both of you to see if it's a right fit. It's an interview.

Be careful of doing any program where you are supposed to change the course of your life and heal your body in less than six months. It took a lifetime to get to the point where you are asking for help, so patience and perseverance are needed over an expanded time frame. You want easy, slow, sustainable change.

Beware of a "one size fits all" approach. Every person is bio-individual. This is why one diet may have worked for your friend, but didn't for you. Good health coaches, like good doctors, take the time to know you down to the smallest detail, in order to create your personal plan.

Prepare to work. Working with your own personal coach is an investment. The investment will pay big dividends by saving you money and sickness down the road. In turn, you will be inspiring and motivating others who watch your progress. Make sure your coach inspires you, and invests in you. It's a two way street. Good coaches don't just spend an hour with their clients twice a month. They think about them in between, do research on unique issues, round up tools in preparation for the next session and spend time creating individualized plans. That one hour that you spend with them is nothing in comparison to the hours they have put into planning your care. In return, it's not enough to pay them. You must do the work on your end too!

Bibliography

"The 92 Percent Clean Plate Club: You're Not Alone in Eating Everything on Your Plate." ScienceDaily. ScienceDaily, n.d. Web. 02 Mar. 2015.

Amen, Daniel G. The Healing ADD Power Program: The Complete Guide to Understanding and Healing Attention Deficit Disorder From Childhood Through Adulthood. Newport Beach, CA: Mind Works, 2005. Print.

Amen, Daniel G. Healing ADD: The Breakthrough Program That Allows You to See and Heal the Six Types of Attention Deficit Disorder. New York: G.P. Putnam's Sons, 2001. Print.

Anand, Preetha, Ajaikumar B. Kunnumakara, Chitra Sundaram, Kuzhuvelil B. Harikumar, Sheeja T. Tharakan, Oiki S. Lai, Bokyung Sung, and Bharat B. Aggarwal. "Cancer Is a Preventable Disease That Requires Major Lifestyle Changes." Pharmaceutical Research. Springer US, n.d. Web. 12 Mar. 2015.

Augustine, E. B. Pusey, and William Benham. The Confessions of St. Augustine. The Imitation of Christ. New York: P.F. Collier, 1909. Print.

"Balanced Living." Self Healing Benefits of Meditation. N.p., n.d. Web. 02 Mar. 2015.

Baun, Jane Ralls. Papers Presented at the Fifteenth International Conference on Patristic Studies Held in Oxford 2007. Leuven: Peeters, 2010. Print.

Blaylock, Russell L. Excitotoxins: The Taste That Kills. Santa Fe, NM: Health, 1998. Print.

"Body Burden: The Pollution in Newborns." Environmental Working Group. N.p., n.d. Web. 02 Mar. 2015.

Buettner, Dan. The Blue Zones: Lessons for Living Longer from the People Who've Lived the Longest. Washington, D.C.: National Geographic Society, 2009. Print.

Cairns, Scott. Idiot Psalms: New Poems. N.p.: Paraclete Poetry, 2014. Print.

CDC. "National Diabetes Statistics Report." Centers for Disease Control and Prevention. Centers for Disease Control and

Prevention, 06 Jan. 2015. Web. 11 Feb. 2015.

"Dormition of the Theotokos Greek Orthodox Church of Oakmont & Verona." Dormition of the Theotokos Greek Orthodox Church of Oakmont & Verona. N.p., n.d. Web. 02 Mar. 2015.

"Environmental Working Group." Environmental Working Group. EWG, n.d. Web. 02 Mar. 2015.

Felix, Marcus Minucius, and G. W. Clarke. The Octavius of Marcus Minucius Felix. New York: Newman, 1974. Print.

"HMS." Mind-body Genomics. Harvard Medical School, n.d. Web. 02 Mar. 2015.

"How to Make Stress Your Friend." Kelly McGonigal:. N.p., n.d. Web. 02 Mar. 2015.

Hyman, Mark. The Blood Sugar Solution: The Ultrahealthy Program for Losing Weight, Preventing Disease, and Feeling Great Now! New York, NY: Little, Brown, 2012. Print.

Hyman, Mark. The Blood Sugar Solution: The Ultrahealthy Program for Losing Weight, Preventing Disease, and Feeling Great Now! New York, NY: Little, Brown, 2012. Print.

Junger, Alejandro. Clean: The Revolutionary Program to Restore the Body's Natural Ability to Heal Itself. San Francisco: HarperOne, 2009. Print.

"Life Transfigured: A Journal of Orthodox Nuns." Orthodox Monastery of the Transfiguration. N.p., n.d. Web. 02 Mar. 2015.

Lipman, Frank, and Mollie Doyle. Revive: Stop Feeling Spent and Start Living Again. New York: Simon & Schuster, 2010. Print.

Louth, Andrew. Early Christian Writings: The Apostolic Fathers. Harmondsworth, Middlesex, England: Penguin, 1987. Print.

Moriarty, P. E. The Life of St. Augustine, Bishop, Confessor and Doctor of the Church. Philadelphia: P.F. Cunningham, 1873. Print.

Myles Coverdale and the English Bible. Sheffield Moor: D.T. Ingham, Printer, n.d. Print.

"Natural Hormone Reduces Stress Hormones In Arguing Couples." ScienceDaily. ScienceDaily, n.d. Web. 02 Mar. 2015.

""Nones" on the Rise." Pew Research Centers Religion Public Life

Project RSS. Pew Research Center, 08 Oct. 2012. Web. 02 Mar. 2015.

"Orthodox Church Quotes." Orthodox Church Quotes. N.p., n.d. Web. 02 Mar. 2015.

Papagiannē, Gavriēlia, D. Geōrgiou, and Helen Anthony. The Ascetic of Love. Athens: Eptalophos, 2000. Print.

Peeke, Pamela, and Mariska Van. Aalst. The Hunger Fix: The Three-stage Solution to Free Yourself From Your Food Addictions For Life. Emmaus, PA: Rodale, 2012. Print.

Perlmutter, David, and Kristin Loberg. Grain Brain: The Surprising Truth About Wheat, Carbs, and Sugar--Your Brain's Silent Killers. N.p.: n.p., n.d. Print.

"Psychology Today." Addiction. N.p., n.d. Web. 01 Mar. 2015.

Rich, S. K. "Reply to B Wansink and CS Wansink." International Journal of Obesity 35.3 (2010): 462. Web.

Rosenthal, Joshua. Integrative Nutrition: The Future of Nutrition. New York City: Institute for Integrative Nutrition, 2006. Print.

"Should I Eat That? How To Choose The Healthiest Foods." Should I Eat That? How To Choose The Healthiest Foods. N.p., n.d. Web. 02 Mar. 2015.

"Silence, Stillness and Listening to God." Wellspring - Reflections in Orthodox Christian Theology. Father John Breck, n.d. Web.

Sophrony, Archimandrite. His Life Is Mine. Crestwood, NY: St. Vladimir's Seminary, 1977. Print.

"Statins Elevate Risk of Diabetes in Postmenopausal Women." Forbes. Forbes Magazine, n.d. Web. 02 Mar. 2015.

Stewart, David. Healing Oils of the Bible. Marble Hill, MO: Center for Aromatherapy Research & Education, 2002. Print.

"Stress Management." Stress Symptoms: Effects on Your Body and Behavior. Mayo Clinic, n.d. Web. 11 Feb. 2015.

Trivieri, Larry. The American Holistic Medical Association Guide to Holistic Health: Healing Therapies for Optimal Wellness. New York: J. Wiley, 2001. Print.

Tsurikov, Vladimir. Philaret, Metropolitan of Moscow, 1782-1867: Perspectives on the Man, His Works, and His Times. Jordanville, NY: Variable, 2003. Print.

Vaillant, George E. Triumphs of Experience: The Men of the Harvard Grant Study. Cambridge, MA: Belknap of Harvard UP, 2012. Print.

Ware, Kallistos. The Collected Works. N.p.: n.p., 2004. Print.

Warren, Richard. The Daniel Plan: 40 Days to a Healthier Life. Grand Rapids, MI: Zondervan, 2013. Print.

About the Author

Cynthia Hopkins Damaskos was born a Southern California girl, but ended up growing up in Oregon. When living in the Los Angeles area just became too nuts, her parents sold everything, loaded up a Volkswagen bug with a few belongings, including a little girl and a little boy, and headed north to Seattle. This decision was based on a television show which portrayed Seattle as being a shining beacon of peace and beauty. Arriving in Seattle in the evening with traffic jams galore (yes, even back in 1968) her dad turned the car around, saying, "I had enough of this in California," and headed south again. The car broke down in Albany, Oregon. The rest is history.

———————— ∽ ————————

Invite Cynthia to Speak to Your Group or Organization

Cynthia is passionate about helping women achieve a balanced life, full of peace and joy, through her work as a health coach, author, and speaker.

Trained as a holistic health coach through The Institute for Integrative Nutrition, her programs facilitate bringing out the best in every woman, while averting and reversing disease through lifestyle changes.

To connect with Cynthia, learn more about her health coaching practice, the Holistic Christian Woman Bootcamp, and other programs, you may go to the following websites:

www.thedamaskosway.com
www.theholisticchristianwoman.com
www.orthodoxspeakers.com

48751276R00092

Made in the USA
Lexington, KY
11 January 2016